The Thirteenth Discipline

The Thirteenth Discipline

Formative and Reformative Discipline in Congregational Life

LIONEL M. MORIAH

WIPF & STOCK · Eugene, Oregon

THE THIRTEENTH DISCIPLINE
Formative and Reformative Discipline in Congregational Life

Copyright © 2011 Lionel M. Moriah. All rights reserved. Except for brief quotations in critical publications or reviews, no part of this book may be reproduced in any manner without prior written permission from the publisher. Write: Permissions, Wipf and Stock Publishers, 199 W. 8th Ave., Suite 3, Eugene, OR 97401.

Wipf & Stock
An Imprint of Wipf and Stock Publishers
199 W. 8th Ave., Suite 3
Eugene, OR 97401
www.wipfandstock.com

ISBN 13: 978-1-61097-062-4

Manufactured in the U.S.A.

Unless otherwise indicated, Scripture quotations are from the Revised Standard Version of the Bible, copyright © 1946, 1952, and 1971. National Council of the Churches of Christ in the United States of America. Used by permission. All rights reserved.

Scripture quotations from *The Message*. Copyright © by Eugene H. Peterson 1993, 1994, 1995, 1996, 2000, 2001, 2002. Used by permission of NavPress Publishing Group.

The author wishes to acknowledge the kind permission of Carters Professional Corporation to quote at length from a number of its publications.

Contents

Foreword vii
Preface ix
Acknowledgments xi
Introduction xiii

1 What is Christian Discipline? Should the Church Practice It? 1

2 Discipline in the Older Testament 10

3 Discipline in the New Testament 22

4 Christian Discipline: Views from the Congregation 33

5 Christian Discipline: Lessons from History 44

6 Matthew 18: Blueprint for Christian Discipline 54

7 Christian Discipline and the Secular Law 66

8 Christian Discipline: Confronting the Tide
     of Modern Western Culture 86

9 Establishing the Ministry of Christian Discipline:
     The First Three Pillars 98

10 Establishing the Ministry of Christian Discipline:
     The Fourth Pillar 112

Afterword 125
Bibliography 129
Scripture Index 133
Subject Index 138

Foreword

In the last two decades, since the Church Growth movement reached its height in North America, several themes have emerged that have spoken to church leaders. Among these are emphases on spiritual renewal and spiritual formation, both of which have focused primarily on the internal spiritual life of the church. The call to build healthy congregations and churches is not the least of the trumpets that have sounded. Authors have penned books enumerating the factors and principles needed to build healthy congregations. You will go far to find a book among them that cites Christian discipline as a characteristic of church health.

But Dr. Lionel Moriah does not simply view Christian discipline as a contributing factor of church health. He helps us appreciate its central importance in the life of the church. Most of us would not expect to find the practice of Christian discipline emerging as central to the modus operandi of a healthy church.

This book combines a scholarly treatment of the topic examining the biblical record, church history, and contemporary church life. In addition, the reader will be offered practical applications one would expect from an experienced church theologian.

Examining the biblical record of what it means to live in God's covenant community, readers are challenged to bring "the other" before one's mind. This comes at a time when the swift current in literature surrounding Christian discipleship and formation is focused on the individual. To live as a follower of Christ is a call to life in covenant community. This brings great privilege, mutuality, and responsibility.

I appreciated Dr. Moriah's emphasis that at the heart of Christian discipline is the goal of restoration when it is at all possible. Citing helpful scenarios, the reader will be encouraged with the positive implications of Christian discipline among a congregation of believers.

The book was birthed from a pastoral practitioner who had the desire to mine the biblical, historical, and contemporary records for the gold of life in covenant Christian community. When all is well in a congregation, that is one reality; this book explores how to approach Christian discipline when all of life is not well and to do it in a God-honoring way.

If you desire an intensive biblical study on this topic, this book will serve you well. If you are looking for practical steps for weaving this emphasis into the life of your congregation, this book will also be helpful for you. If you need a better understanding of Christian discipline, you too will be blessed.

I have heard it said that "to belong to Jesus is to belong to everyone else who belongs to Jesus." Dr. Moriah's book enables the reader to realize that the very fabric of Christian discipline is not an add-on to the development of a healthy church or congregation. It is in fact part of God's DNA for His people.

Dr. Harry G. Gardner
President
Dean of Theology
Professor of Church Leadership
Acadia Divinity College
Wolfville, Nova Scotia

Preface

IN THIS WORK, I argue for the restoration or revitalization of Christian discipline as a fundamental, biblically mandated, and essential ministry in healthy Christian congregations, and seek to offer practical advice to churches on how it might be carried out. The book's foundation is my thesis, *Christian Discipline: Legalism or Covenant Responsibility?*, submitted to the Doctor of Ministry program at Acadia Divinity College in 1997. That work was grounded in biblical study, in my seventeen years of pastoral experience in Baptist churches in Atlantic Canada, on primary qualitative research, and on a survey of relevant secondary literature. In preparing this manuscript, I have sought to update the material, bringing to it a further thirteen years of pastoral experience and six years' experience teaching seminary students. I have also, where appropriate, canvassed current literature on various aspects of the subject.

The title, *The Thirteenth Discipline*, is a deliberate reference to Richard Foster's landmark *Celebration of Discipline*, a work in which he explores twelve practices through whose intentional cultivation Christians may come to experience the fullness of the Christian life. Foster refers to them as "classical disciplines," which he believes are "central to experiential Christianity"[1]—i.e., they are practices all Christians should build into the fabric of their daily lives. Foster groups the disciplines into three sets: Under the rubric of inward disciplines he discusses meditation, prayer, fasting, and study. The four he calls outward disciplines are simplicity, solitude, submission, and service. Finally, he describes four corporate disciplines—confession, worship, guidance, and celebration. I hope to persuade readers that Christian discipline is an appropriate, indeed, a necessary addition to this last set: Christian discipline can make a significant impact on the lives of individual Christians, and through the serious, committed effort of faithful congregations, the formative and

---

1. Richard J. Foster, *Celebration of Discipline*, 1 (FN).

reformative power of Christian discipline can demonstrate to the world the wonder of God's transforming grace.

I have three hopes for this book: First, that its contents might go some way toward satisfying the church's current need for resources to support the practice of sound Christian discipline. Second, that it might stimulate further research and diligent pursuit of ways in which churches can exercise discipline faithfully, courageously, and lovingly, in keeping with the biblical witness. Finally, I hope that the discussion it contains and the resources it provides will assist and support all involved in the ministry of the church who struggle in this post-modern world, where—to paraphrase a colleague—"a culture of fear of giving offense" may well be the greatest obstacle to the practice of Christian discipline and the healthy growth of the local congregation. I hope readers will find the treatment of the subject both scholarly and sensitive to the needs of the contemporary church, and the resources offered both practical and friendly to those who would use them.

Lionel Moriah
Halifax, Nova Scotia
April 2011

Acknowledgments

Sincere appreciation is expressed to several individuals who have played significant roles in the production of this book. First and foremost, though, I am deeply grateful to God for the privilege and provision afforded me from the inception to the completion of this project. Beyond the provision of intellectual, mental, physical, as well as spiritual and material resources was the indispensable presence of several people without whom I could not have reached this stage.

My beloved wife, Jemell, has been a tremendous support and partner on each step of the journey. Her support has taken the form of the sacrifice of time together during the demanding periods of research and other activities necessary to the writing process. I am deeply indebted to her for allowing me the time and space, and for offering her insights while I struggled to make this a reader-friendly book.

The original inspiration for this book based on my thesis came from Dr. Robert Wilson, my Doctor of Ministry thesis supervisor, which makes this declaration of gratitude more than a decade overdue. I am grateful for his ongoing encouragement which kept the possibility of this project alive. My sincere gratitude also goes to Reverend Joseph Manchester, ministry mentor during my DMin. His diligence kept me focused on the goal of excellence.

My editor, Lorraine Street, carried the bulk of the "potter's task" of taking the original manuscript and shaping it into the current form. This result comes at great sacrifice to her, and I am grateful for her efforts.

My ultimate hope is that we may all benefit from the fruits of this research in attaining a clearer vision for the work of God through the local church as well as in the wider kingdom. Indeed, to God belongs the credit and glory for whatever enlightenment and insights I have gained from ministry in local churches and have tried to bring to this resource. I hope it will be of use to them.

Introduction

A PARABLE OF AND FOR OUR TIMES...

THE PASTOR SETTLED INTO her new charge with great enthusiasm and a lofty vision. The prospects and possibilities seemed boundless. All went well until the personal situation of a member of the congregation was brought to her attention. Clarke (as we shall call him) was involved in an adulterous relationship. The pastor believed that such a relationship was obviously, explicitly, and unequivocally condemned by Jesus. The situation was not new—the relationship had begun before she became pastor—but what she saw as a critical issue of moral failure had apparently not been addressed by her predecessor. Nor had it been acknowledged by the congregation, other than in its acceptance of Clarke's voluntary resignation from a position of leadership. In the congregation's records, the pastor found Clarke's letter: It appeared to be an admission of guilt and an acknowledgment that his situation disqualified him from holding office in the church. The congregation's Board of Deacons had responded to it, expressing the hope that Clarke would resolve the situation properly and return to active fellowship. Nothing else, however, had been done by the previous pastor or by any other church leader acting in an official capacity.

The new pastor hoped that, through her pastoral care efforts, Clarke might be encouraged to repent and be restored to the congregation. The matter was, however, not to be so easily resolved. Initially, Clarke responded positively to both pastoral care and professional counseling. He renewed his interest in the church and appeared to be attempting to reconcile with his wife. Things looked promising. He began attending worship and taking an interest in business meetings again. After a period of two years, however, it was discovered that he had not severed his adulterous relationship, and the situation came to a head when he nevertheless expressed interest in joining the choir, voting at business meetings, and taking communion, and when other members of the congregation supported his desire to do so.

The pastor met with him, encouraged him to make a clear statement of repentance before the congregation, to express his desire for God's forgiveness and that of the congregation, and to end the relationship. He was also encouraged to join a Bible study group as an aid to spiritual growth, and to consider further professional counseling. Unfortunately, he chose instead to continue the relationship and once again to minimize his involvement with the congregation.

Some time later, Clarke became involved in a second adulterous relationship that resulted in the breakup of a family. The pastor once again tried to address the situation with him through pastoral care. She also discussed the situation with the congregation's lay leaders. Some categorically rejected the biblical principle of Christian discipline—and its potential consequence of restoration to or exclusion from Church membership depending on the response of the one being disciplined—declaring it to be "judgmental," "out of step with the times," and potentially disruptive to the congregation. It also seemed clear that others would rather the conduct be ignored than addressed; indeed, some members made it plain that they would prefer the pastor's resignation to Clarke's removal from the fellowship, should it come to a choice between the two.

A number of individuals, however, did agree that the situation should be addressed in light of biblical principles and precedents. Eventually, the Board of Deacons decided that the matter should be brought to the congregation for discussion, and it was placed on the agenda of the upcoming quarterly business meeting. The discussion never took place, however, because Clarke submitted a letter beforehand, indicating that he was withdrawing from the fellowship of the church until his life was in order.

It appeared that Clarke, at some level, recognized that he did not know or understand the biblical teachings relevant to these matters, nor their formative and reformative implications, and he wrote that he wished someone had approached him much earlier with such spiritual counsel. Nonetheless, he rejected or ignored further attempts on the part of the pastor, and her efforts at Christian discipline in this matter prompted a vote of confidence about her leadership. Although the vote of the congregants affirmed her conduct, the entire situation had such damaging effects that she resigned not long afterward.

THE LESSON OF THIS PARABLE

The issue of discipline is not an easy one for most Christian congregations. Given the individualism that runs so deep in modern (and post-modern) Western culture, many people find it difficult to accept the notion that we, as individuals, are responsible to others in matters relating to our beliefs and, especially, our actions. Congregations, for their part, often do not want to sit in judgment of individuals or enforce standards among their members. But the evidence of Scripture and the precedents of Church history, some of which will be discussed in these pages, show that this ministry is important both for the glory of God and the credibility of the missional church. The parable related above illustrates some of the damage that can be done to relationships in the church when Christian discipline is ignored, neglected, mishandled, or rejected. In the discussion that follows, the writer intends to show that Christian discipline is a ministry with solid biblical and historical warrant and foundations, and that it is as relevant and important to the church today as it ever was.

CHRISTIAN DISCIPLINE AND RELATIONSHIP

The ministry of biblical or Christian discipline (commonly called "church discipline") is a matter of both prevention and formation and of correction and reformation, and it is best appreciated and understood within the context of relationship. Scripture has much to say about discipline, often in the context of the relationship of parents and children, but also about God disciplining his people on the basis of the covenant between them. Here, I believe, lies the foundation on which the church bases, and can build—or re-build—its understanding and practice of Christian discipline.

As will be outlined below, in the older biblical Testament we see that God intentionally initiated a relationship with a people, desiring to adopt them and bless them, and that God asked them, in return, for their love and obedience to his will. If and when the people disobeyed the commandments of God, they reaped the negative consequences of judgment, to be sure, but even these consequences were designed by God, in his boundless love for his people, to prompt and promote repentance among them and their eventual restoration to himself.

The New Testament likewise recounts instances whereby the early church sought to preserve its unique character and witness as the people of God by practicing the ministry of Christian discipline within its ranks. In every case, the context of such practice was the covenant or communal relationship of mutual accountability that bound the members together. Thus, the writer of the Epistle to the Hebrews linked this practice to God's design for a people adopted as children into the divine family, children called to reflect the divine image as Christ embodied it: "He [Christ] reflects the glory of God and bears the very stamp of his nature, upholding the universe by his word of power" (Heb 1:3).

This study and discussion of the biblical concept of discipline is thus grounded in the biblical concept of covenant. It presents discipline as an essential covenant responsibility, one whose right practice is indispensable to the health of congregations. The primary goal of this book is to endorse and promote discipline within the local church as an important and proper ministry of formation and training as well as reformation, correction, and restoration—i.e., practiced for the prevention of problems and their resolution—particularly where recurring sin threatens the health, growth, and effectual functioning of the congregation. There are many examples of the practice of Christian discipline in communities over the centuries. This book will include brief glimpses at discipline as practiced in a number of them, in particular, the church in Calvin's Geneva and in nineteenth-century Atlantic Canada.

As the parable recounted above illustrates, discipline is often an unpopular subject in Christian churches. Is it because of ignorance or a lack of understanding of the biblical mandate? Is it that people are resistant to the implications of their calls to be disciples of Christ? Is it fear? Fear of being judged oneself and found wanting? Fear of hurting other people? Fear of unleashing something unmanageable if difficult issues are addressed?

The rampant culture of individualism, as well as the prevailing emphasis on human rights and personal freedom, and the growing litigiousness in many Western countries suggest other reasons for this fear: Indeed, why many congregations hesitate to insist on discipline within their membership is not a mystery. Therefore, this book will also suggest ways congregations may practice biblical discipline both courageously and in relative "safety," primarily through the sound application of biblical teachings in the development of and adherence to their fundamental covenants and constitutions, and in the creation and establishment of sound risk management practices that will help minimize churches' exposure to legal liability.[2]

The author hopes that the evidence marshaled and arguments made here will aid in the establishment of new approaches to, or the revision of current practices in, Christian discipline. Devotional material and questions for personal or group study have been added at the end of each chapter to stimulate thinking and discussion—and, no doubt, further questions—on these matters.

---

2. While most of the material in this book is general enough to apply and be used anywhere, some information is specifically related to the current state of the law in Canada.

1

What is Christian Discipline? Should the Church Practice It?

WHAT IS CHRISTIAN DISCIPLINE?

According to the *World Book Dictionary*, the semantic range of the English word "discipline" includes the following definitions: (1) training of the mind or character; (2) the training effect of experience, misfortune, or other happenings; (3) a trained condition of order and obedience; (4) order kept among pupils, soldiers, or members of any group; (5) a particular system of rules for conduct; (6) punishment, chastisement; (7) a branch of education or instruction; (8) methods or rules for regulating the conduct of members of a church; (9) control exercised over members of a church.[1]

"In its most general sense, discipline refers to systematic instruction given to a disciple. This sense also preserves the origin of the word, which is Latin, *disciplina*, 'instruction,' from the root *discere*, 'to learn,' and from which *discipulus*, 'disciple, pupil' also derives."[2] The word thus denotes the process of personal character formation of an individual in subjection to a master or system of study, as illustrated in the disciples' relationship with Jesus: the formation of their characters was guided by his precepts and practices. By extension, discipline is a name given to the formal system of laws and directions intended to shape the private and public conduct of the church's disciples—those being formed—and it

---

1. *The World Book Dictionary*, s.v. "Discipline," accessed October 16, 2006, http://www.worldbook.com/wb/dict?lu=a&cl=3>.

2. *Wikipedia*, s.v. "Discipline," accessed July 29, 2008, http://en.wikipedia.org/wiki/Discipline.

includes training in such matters as the liturgical (worship) and pastoral care (service) practices of congregations and ministers or priests.[3]

In addition to its formative aspect, discipline also carries a reformative connotation, as seen in a number of the definitions outlined above: e.g., discipline means "punishment, chastisement" or "methods or rules for regulating the conduct of members of a church." The Hebrew and Greek words usually translated "discipline" are also sometimes rendered "chastise" in English translations of Scripture,[4] and that word certainly makes the corrective or reformative element of discipline more explicit. Discipline as chastisement may be described this way: "Church discipline is a response of an ecclesiastical body to some perceived wrong, whether in action or in doctrine. Its most extreme form in modern churches is excommunication where the offender is banished from the church community until such time as he or she repents or recants. Along with preaching and proper administration of the sacraments, Protestants during the Reformation considered it one of the marks of a true church."[5]

SHOULD THE CHURCH PRACTICE CHRISTIAN DISCIPLINE?

This is often where congregational conversations about Christian discipline—if they ever take place—begin and end. As has been noted, there is far from universal agreement that the ministry of Christian discipline should be exercised at all within the body of Christ. People who think it out of place usually raise one or more of the following overlapping objections: (1) Jesus always forgave sinners; (2) Jesus did not commission his church to practice internal discipline; and (3) Jesus decreed that the wheat and the tares should be left alone to grow together. Let us look at each of these objections in turn.

---

3. *The Catholic Encyclopedia*, s.v. "Discipline," accessed July 29, 2008, http://www.newadvent.org/cathen/05030a.htm.

4. For example, in Lev 26:23, the word translated into Latin as *disciplina* is the Hebrew word *yasar*, which means "to instruct, warn, rebuke." The Hebrew word *musar* is also often translated into English as "discipline, instruction," as in the "chastisement for our healing" spoken of in Isa 53:5.

5. *Wikipedia*, s.v. "Church Discipline," accessed July 29, 2008, http://en.wikipedia.org/wiki/Churchdiscipline.

Objection 1: "Jesus always forgave sinners."

The claim is often put this way: "Jesus never taught or modeled Christian discipline. He always demonstrated forgiveness toward those who were guilty of any offence." Jesus' treatment of the woman caught in adultery, recounted in John 8:1–11, is usually cited as evidence of his purportedly lax view on moral issues. The fact that Jesus did not declare that she was innocent, that he pointedly directed her to stop what she was doing—". . . go, and do not sin again" (v. 11)—is often ignored in popular discussions of the passage, although commentators generally agree that Jesus acted here with *both* judgment and the merciful grace of forgiveness.

While many think the passage is the work of a redactor and not that of the original gospel writer,[6] it is nevertheless accepted as paradigmatic of Jesus' attitude toward moral behavior, in that his actions were balanced ". . . between truth on the one side, by which he condemns the woman's sin, and grace on the other, with which he withholds condemnation from the woman herself."[7] In addition, in his response to the actions of the Pharisees and the crowd, Jesus pointedly, if tacitly, condemns their wrongheaded application of community discipline. He challenges their misapplication of Scripture, for the Mosaic law as set out in Leviticus (20:10) and Deuteronomy (22:22–24) called for both participants in adultery to be punished. He also realizes that this situation is less about the woman than it is an attempt to trap him, and he refuses to be drawn: His response to the question of the religious leaders—"Now in the law Moses commanded us to stone such. What do you say about her?"(John 8:5)—challenges the crowd directly by forcing its members to acknowledge the universality of sin: "Let him who is without sin among you be the first to throw a stone at her" (8:7b), and he appeals directly to the Deuteronomic passages, which say that ". . . those who witness a crime and bring home a successful accusation must then be the first to stone the victim. But the accusers must engage in self-examination."[8] Jesus thus illuminates the hypocritical and dangerously biased practice of judging others without at the same time judging ourselves, a phenom-

---

6. Blum, "John," 302, 346–47.

7. Ellis, "The Gospel According to John," 1334. Others suggest that it is John's intention to portray Jesus as ". . . more concerned with the rehabilitation of the sinner than with seeing the Law meticulously satisfied." See "The Gospel According to John," *Wycliffe Bible Commentary*, 1090.

8. Burge, "Gospel of John," 93.

enon all too often present when discipline is misapplied, as it is here: There has been no trial; the woman has been summarily judged and is being publicly humiliated and punished as if she, alone, has sinned.

The Pharisees are attempting to embarrass Jesus, but they succeed only in embarrassing themselves as not one was able to claim to be sinless. Furthermore, they expose their gender bias—why is the male partner of the woman not being punished?—their complete lack of compassion for the woman—they could have brought her to Jesus privately, not in public—and ultimately their indifference to the spiritual well-being of the community, which is always affected by the sin of any member: They do not respond to Jesus or minister to the crowd; they simply drop the stones and scatter.

To be sure, the story demonstrates Jesus' compassion toward the woman who sins. That does not mean, however, that he ignores or condones her sin: he does not. He bluntly condemns it, and in the clearest of terms, as we see in the language of the King James Version: "Go and sin no more." Here Jesus demonstrates that a clear call to *metanoia*— that is, to a change of heart and mind and behavior, in other words, to repentance—and compassion on the part of the authority (in this case himself) are both required in such a situation, and he effectively endorses the process he outlines elsewhere (i.e., in Matt 18:15–22) as the way Christians should deal with sin committed by a fellow Christian. In that passage, Jesus exhorts his followers to deal with sin in the community, not to pretend it doesn't exist. He describes how his followers should do this and, in strong language, instructs them about what they are to do if someone "refuses to listen even to the church" (v. 17), while nevertheless enjoining his disciples to forgive "seventy times seven" times (v. 22). This passage is placed between the parable of the lost sheep (Matt 18:12–14) and the parable of the unforgiving slave (Matt 18:23–35), underscoring that the context and purpose of disciplinary efforts is reconciliation between persons and restoration of right relationship between human beings and God—i.e., restoration of humans to their position as children of God, heirs to the covenant, those who do his will.

Thus does Augustine interpret the story of the woman caught in adultery told in John 8, arguing that Jesus is contending here for the exercise of courageous action and loving commiseration in the exercise of the pastoral responsibility for spiritual care. Augustine echoes the appeal for balance in dealing with the realities of sinful conduct of church members by pastoral leaders, as the following comment on his own outlines:

> As Augustine noted . . . we are in danger from both hope and despair. That is, we can have a false optimism that says "God is merciful so I can do as I please" or a despair that says "there is no forgiveness for the sin I have committed." This story shows we should keep these two inclinations in balance. There is no sin that God does not forgive. Christ's death atoned for all sin. The only sin that remains unforgiven is the one that is not repented of. But, on the other hand, God's call to us is to intimacy with himself, and sin cannot be in his presence any more than darkness can be in the presence of light. Christ's atonement cleanses us from sin as we repent day by day, and his Spirit is working in us a transformation so that in the end we will come out pure, though not in this life (1 Jn 1:8). But sin must be cut off. We must take it seriously. Jesus himself often tells us to fear God and his judgment.[9]

Augustine here speaks of the reality of God's forgiveness and compassion, while he also emphasizes, in no uncertain terms, that the community of the faithful must deal with sin in its midst. In so doing, he echoes the admonitions of Paul in his letter to the Corinthians (1 Cor 5; 12:24–26; 2 Cor 2). Paul says to them: "Your boasting is not good. Do you not know that a little leaven leavens the whole lump?" (1 Cor 5:6). His metaphor suggests that sin (even a little) is like yeast, which, if allowed to, will spread throughout the whole and may destroy the individual and the entire community: sin ignored (or handled badly as the Pharisees do in John 8) infects and affects the whole community. It is important to remember that ". . . Jesus is not implying the woman's innocence with his final words ("Then neither do I condemn you"), rather his sovereignty to forgive sins is displayed (Mark 2:5 ff). The story's crisp ending captures the seriousness with which Jesus viewed sin and judgment—even the sin of those who accuse the woman—and his gracious, forgiving outlook on those who are caught in its grip."[10]

From the actions of Jesus described in John 8 and from Paul's admonitions in his epistles to the Corinthians, it is possible to extrapolate a number of principles that should ground and shape the disciplinary actions and processes of congregations, whose members must always remember that they are called upon to act compassionately toward the

---

9. *IVP New Testament Commentaries*, s.v. "Jesus Forgives a Woman Taken in Adultery," accessed March 15, 2011, http://www.biblegateway.com/resources/commentaries/IVP-NT/John/Jesus-Forgives-Woman-Taken.

10. Burge, "Gospel of John," 93–94.

individual, with the goal always being the reconciliation of persons and restoration of the individual to fellowship, for the sake of both the individual and the entire body.

(1) Churches must intentionally exercise what might be called a "ministry of prevention," i.e., they must recognize that they have a moral obligation to give guidance to those vulnerable to sin—that is, to everyone, including themselves—through admonition and teaching and forgiveness (See Matt 26:41; 1 Cor 5:1–11; 2 Cor 2:10–11).

(2) The processes and actions used by churches must be unbiased and fair in dealing with sinful conduct: they must seek to bring all parties involved in the actions to account insofar as they have the authority to do so (See 1 Cor 5:12–13).

(3) Congregations should avoid publicly embarrassing the wrongdoer, an act that not only isolates the sinner but has a negative effect on the whole community (See Matt 18:15–17; contrast 1 Cor 5:3–5).

(4) The congregation, especially those in leadership positions, must undertake serious personal spiritual reflection and self-examination so as to avoid establishing or modeling double standards and other hypocritical responses to sinful behavior (See 1 Cor 5:2).

(5) Jesus must be the model for this delicate ministry: though sovereign, he nevertheless dealt graciously with sinful humankind: His mission in miniature, might it be said? "For such a one this punishment by the majority is enough; so you should rather turn to forgive and comfort him, or he may be overwhelmed by excessive sorrow. So I beg you to reaffirm your love for him" (2 Cor 2:6–8).

Objection 2: "Jesus did not commission his church to practice internal discipline."

A second argument raised by those who strenuously reject Christian discipline as an appropriate ministry of the church is that Jesus spent his time teaching positive life lessons, as in the Sermon on the Mount, and not pronouncing prohibitions against negative behavior. This position, however, must be informed by, and balanced with, reference to passages which recount Jesus' evidently realistic understanding of the propensity of human beings to sin—with the consequent rupturing of the divine-human relationship and of relationships between and among people—

and of those things necessary to regulate behavior. Thus, discipline, as demonstrated by Jesus' admonition to the woman to go and sin no more (echoed in Matt 9:1–8, Mark 2:3–12, Luke 5:18–26, and 7:36–50), should be seen as a positive and formative aspect of the Christian life, i.e., it is an encouragement and exhortation of the erring saint to repent (that is, to turn and return) to the accepted standard of behavior and thus to be restored to intimacy with God. Although Jesus did indeed proffer forgiveness, he clearly and simultaneously insisted on repentance as one of the principal standards of faithful discipleship.

Objection 3. "Jesus said the wheat and the tares should be left together."

Still others contend that Jesus promoted a kingdom ethic that encourages, or at least permits, "the wheat and the tares" to grow and thrive together until they are separated at the final judgment (Matt 13:24–33). The argument runs that Jesus hereby rejected the notion that his followers should practice reformative or corrective discipline that would separate the wheat from the tares. Unfortunately, this principle, which might be called pious procrastination, seems to be based on the faulty notion that the church and the kingdom are identical in the so-called "kingdom parables" of Matthew 13. In addition, many have argued that this objection is inconsistent with the substance of Jesus' teachings elsewhere, not least elsewhere in Matthew's gospel itself:

> Jesus observed these principles [of practicing discipline within the church for the benefit of its own inner purity, even while it remains part of the world where evil is prevalent] when he embraced sinners at table fellowship and denounced the Pharisees; but the twin principle of proffered forgiveness and personal repentance offers abundant applications for Jesus' followers as well. Jesus' primary point is the coexistence of kingdom people with the world's people in this age. Though the context also suggests some application to the church (Mt 13:19–23, 47–50), the point here is not that we should abandon efforts to keep the church pure (Mt 18:7–14, 21–35). Moreover, the point is that the kingdom remains obscure in the present world and only the final day will bring God's true children into their vindicated glory and banish the wicked from among them.[11]

11. *IVP New Testament Commentary*, s.v. "The Coming Separation," accessed March 15, 2011, http://www.biblegateway.com/resources/commentaries/IVP-NT/Matt/Coming-Separation-750.

CHRISTIAN DISCIPLINE: BIBLICAL WARRANT AND BIBLICAL MODELS

The propositions on church discipline offered in this book rest on the conviction that its practice by the people of God throughout the church age *is* biblically mandated, and that church discipline is also indicative of—i.e., it foreshadows—the final judgment. Rather than yielding to the temptation of such extremes as careless compromise or callous condemnation, Christian leaders are encouraged to search the Scriptures for the appropriate postures and principles of compassionate formation and correction modeled by our Lord and Savior, Jesus Christ. The greatest challenge to the effective establishment and practice of Christian discipline in congregations may well be that of encouraging people to view it as a *positive* ministry from which the entire faith community can benefit: clearly, universal support for the ministry would allow for greater impact and effectiveness.

In this effort, the modern church might look to, and draw strength and inspiration from, the example of the Reformed Church in sixteenth-century Geneva. The practice of Christian discipline was intrinsic to its efforts to enable and foster the spiritual, moral, social, and communal formation and transformation of its congregations. The situation has been described this way:

> [T]he ministers and elders remained committed to a vision of pastoral care that included mediating conflicts and restraining violence. The objective was more than modifying behavior, however. Even as they sought the purity of Christ's Church, the Genevan pastors endeavored to provide assistance and guidance for the people of God as they struggled with personal sin and plodded along the pilgrim's path of repentance, forgiveness, and restoration ... Geneva's ministers were not idealists seeking to establish a perfect spiritual commonwealth. Rather, they were open-eyed realists committed to interjecting biblical standards of belief and behavior into the profound messiness of human life so as to make possible Christian forgiveness and salvation. . . . *church discipline was an important expression of pastoral care* . . .[12] (Emphasis added.)

---

12. Manetsch, "Pastoral Care East of Eden," 312–13.

FOR FURTHER REFLECTION . . .

Meditation

This is God's Word on the subject: "As soon as Babylon's seventy years are up and not a day before, I'll show up and take care of you as I promised and bring you back home. I know what I'm doing. I have it all planned out—plans to take care of you, not abandon you, plans to give you the future you hope for. (Jer 29:10,11 *The Message*)

Thought

Prayer is far-reaching in its influence and world-wide in its effects. It affects all men, affects them everywhere, and affects them in all things. It touches man's interest in time and eternity. It lays hold upon God and moves Him to interfere in the affairs of earth.[13]

Questions for Personal and Group Reflection

(1) Discuss the primary meanings of the word "discipline."

(2) What are your views of discipline in the church? Explain whether they are different from your views about discipline in sports teams or in other organizations.

(3) Do you agree or disagree with the objections to the practice of Christian discipline described in this chapter? Which? Why?

---

13. E. M. Bounds, *The Essentials of Prayer*, 57.

2

Discipline in the Older Testament

COVENANT AS CONTEXT FOR DISCIPLINE

THE STARTING POSITION OF these reflections is that any and every discussion of Christian discipline must be framed within the context of relationship, ultimately within the context of the covenant relationship between God and humanity announced and chronicled in the Scriptures. This chapter moves from that vantage point and will canvass the biblical evidence in the Older Testament, which clearly illustrates that covenant people are those who are guided by formative and reformative discipline in order that they might maintain or be restored to their relationship with God and reconciled with each other.

In the Older Testament, the Hebrew word *berith*, most commonly rendered "covenant" in English translations, has three primary uses. First, it is the name given to Yahweh's unilateral promise in Genesis 9, a covenant with no requirement for reciprocity from its beneficiaries (Gen 9:9). This type of relationship is characteristic of covenants made between unequal parties—e.g., a king and his vassals—or, as in this case, between God and all people, here personified by Noah.[1] Second, *berith* is used to describe the explicit terms of an agreement in a partnership of equality (Gen 21:31–32; 26:28–29; 1 Kgs 5:12).[2] A third use of *berith* includes elements of the first two and describes Yahweh's relationship with his chosen people: Although obviously not equal to him in any way, they

1. McComiskey, *The Covenants of Promise*, 62.

2. Ibid., 63. Dumbrell, *Covenant and Creation*, 17–18, cites examples of covenant relationships during the patriarchal period; e.g., between Abraham and Abimelech (Gen 21:21–32) and Isaac and Abimelech (Gen 26:26–33). Payne, *Theology of the Older Testament*, 79, points out the symmetrically bilateral nature of the covenants and their benefits and obligations.

are yet the objects of his grace and are chosen to be in a relationship of mutuality with him. In this covenant, Yahweh acts out of a self-imposed obligation to deliver the people from sin and bondage through ". . . a divine administration of grace and promise,"[3] and he stipulates what, in turn, is expected of them:

> For you are a people holy to the Lord your God; the LORD your God has chosen you to be a people for his own possession, out of all the peoples that are on the face of the earth. It was not because you were more in number than any other people that the LORD set his love upon you and chose you, for you were the fewest of all peoples; but it is because the LORD loves you, and is keeping the oath which he swore to your fathers, that the LORD has brought you out with a mighty hand, and redeemed you from the house of bondage, from the hand of Pharaoh king of Egypt. Know therefore that the LORD your God is God, the faithful God who keeps covenant and steadfast love with those who love him and keep his commandments, to a thousand generations, and requites to their face those who hate him, by destroying them; he will not be slack with him who hates him, he will requite him to his face. You shall therefore be careful to do the commandment, and the statutes, and the ordinances, which I command you this day. And because you hearken to these ordinances, and keep and do them, the LORD your God will keep with you the covenant and the steadfast love which he swore to your fathers to keep; he will love you, bless you, and multiply you; he will also bless the fruit of your body and the fruit of your ground, your grain and your wine and your oil, the increase of your cattle and the young of your flock, in the land which he swore to your fathers to give you. You shall be blessed above all peoples; there shall not be male or female barren among you, or among your cattle. And the LORD will take away from you all sickness; and none of the evil diseases of Egypt, which you knew, will he inflict upon you, but will lay them upon all who hate you (Deut 7:6–15).

For their part, as illustrated in the passage above, the people of God were subject to certain stipulations intended to nurture their relationship with God: Blessings would come through human obedience and divine faithfulness. It is within this aspect of the covenant relationship that discipline is best understood—stipulations emerge from the relationship, which they strengthen and formalize. As some would frame it, God's claim on Israel forms the legal basis for both God's demands

3. Dumbrell, *Covenant and Creation*, 63.

upon as well as discipline of his chosen people.⁴ These covenant provisions were binding, formative, and authoritative.⁵ There is, however, a choice to be made (Deut 30:15–20)⁶: The obedience of the people of Yahweh resulted in their life, health, and well-being, whereas disobedience brought separation from the covenant and, ultimately, death. In this context, the Decalogue sets out and codifies the rules of ethical conduct that are binding on those within the covenant. While delineating ways of translating faith into action, it was also designed for the measurement and maintenance of covenant experience: "The ultimate relationship in which the demand is to be set is the covenant relationship arising from creation. Within that relationship the particular Sinai covenant functions as a sub-set."⁷ The meal commonly eaten at the ratification of a covenant relationship symbolized the intimacy of that relationship, while the stipulations of the covenant regulated it.⁸

Furthermore, *berith* is ultimately the focus of the ministry, i.e., the teaching, of the Prophets, Psalms, and Wisdom literature, in that they appeal to Yahweh's covenant relationship with his people as the sole basis of the requirements of obedience and repentance.⁹ The covenant relationship is the backdrop of all prophetic appeals addressing the often precarious, apostate condition of the nation, and of their calls for a return to loyalty to Yahweh.¹⁰ As representatives of Yahweh, the prophets and prophetesses frequently challenged the nation to live up to its covenant responsibilities.

THE COVENANT AS A MARRIAGE

The distinctively monotheistic nature of the covenant set the religion of Israel apart from contemporary polytheistic religions,¹¹ even as it reinforced the personal character of the relationship that would be regulated by Yahweh according to Israel's obedience or disobedience.¹² In his ap-

---

4. Youngblood, *Heart of the Old Testament*, 42; Childs, *Biblical Theology of the Old and New Testaments*, 138; Bright, *A History of Israel*, 150.

5. Bright, *A History of Israel*, 150, 172.

6. Neff, "Healing the Body of Christ," 35–36.

7. LaSor, *Old Testament Survey*, 91–92.

8. Ibid., 94.

9. Clements, *Prophecy and Covenant*, 16–18.

10. Ibid., 25–26.

11. Hillers, *Covenant* 16, 92, 95.

12. Eichrodt, *Theology of the Old Testament*, 41.

peal for repentance and restoration, the prophet Ezekiel used the marriage metaphor to describe the intimate personal character of the covenant relationship between Yahweh and the chosen people: "I plighted my troth to you and entered into a covenant with you, says the Lord God, and you became mine" (Ezek 16:8). Hosea advances the same metaphor, stressing Yahweh's persistent love, the significance of which has been described this way: "God himself initiated the relationship and . . . He did so at a specific time in history . . . The Lord wooed His people to Himself during the redemptive experience connected with the Exodus, and sealed the resulting marriage by means of the Sinaitic covenant."[13]

Moreover, God makes clear, from his side, the inviolable nature of the relationship: "I will betroth you to me forever; I will betroth you to me in righteousness and justice, in steadfast love, and in mercy. I will betroth you to me in faithfulness; and you shall know the Lord" (Hos 2:19–20). Commentators have seen in the use of this metaphor an unmistakable effort to emphasize the seriousness of the divine-human bond, asserting, for example, that "[l]ike the marriage covenant, the relationship between Yahweh and his people is a covenant of mutual love and trust. Like adultery, apostasy breaks the relationship by despising the love on which it is based, violating the trust, and treating the person as unworthy of exclusive and all-consuming commitment."[14] Employing this metaphor, Ezekiel writes: "Adulterous wife, who receives strangers instead of her husband!" (Ezek 16:32)[15]

Israel's covenant with Yahweh seems unique among covenants common to the times, given the absence of divine witnesses,[16] although clear stipulations as to the responsibilities of each party are identified. The mutuality of the covenant is apparent in that its parties each possess certain freedoms. Yahweh took the initiative in establishing and proposing the covenant but appeals to the willingness and freedom of Israel to choose obedience.[17] Yahweh again bound himself to Israel at Sinai and through subsequent covenant events that either deepened or

---

13. Youngblood, *Heart of the Old Testament*, 55.
14. LaSor, *Old Testament Survey*, 186.
15. Use of the marriage metaphor to speak of the covenant between God and humanity and of the reality and consequences of disobedience and unfaithfulness is carried on in the New Testament. See, e.g., Jas 4:4.
16. Hillers, *Covenant*, 52.
17. Ibid., 65.

re-established relationships between himself, Israel, and other groups.[18] Arguably, this continual covenant renewal and development also allowed later generations to learn for themselves the nature of the people's relationship with Yahweh:

> When your son asks you in time to come, "What is the meaning of the testimonies and the statutes and the ordinances which the LORD our God has commanded you?" then you shall say to your son, "We were Pharaoh's slaves in Egypt; and the LORD brought us out of Egypt with a mighty hand; and the LORD showed signs and wonders, great and grievous, against Egypt and against Pharaoh and all his household before our eyes; and he brought us out from there that he might bring us in and give us the land which he swore to give to our fathers. And the LORD commanded us to do all these statutes, to fear the LORD our God, for our good always, that he might preserve us alive, as at this day. And it will be righteousness for us, if we are careful to do all this commandment before the LORD our God, as he commanded us" (Deut 6:20–25).

Even where the *berith* is not specifically mentioned, the elements of the particular relationship between Yahweh and his people reveal its covenant basis and the presence of a ". . . powerful divine Guardian."[19] The explicitly divine initiative entailed a call to a ". . . relationship of trust and security, based on demand and promise"[20] as well as a call to obedience. This formative thrust of the covenant shows God's benign disposition towards his people, even as it includes the possibility for the imposition of reformative discipline: the ultimate aim is the molding of a people into Yahweh's likeness.[21]

The evidence of the Older Testament seems clear: covenant stipulations aimed at the preservation of the relationship between Yahweh and his people contained both formative and reformative principles. Out of God's boundless and unending love for his people and his desire for their best interests, he taught Israel what was expected of her, that is, God employed formative discipline. When Israel disobeyed, thus failing to be formed by the stipulations of the covenant, reformative discipline was implemented to correct the problem and restore the relationship.

18. Ibid., 146.
19. Eichrodt, *Theology of the Old Testament*, 36–37.
20. Ibid., 41.
21. McComiskey, *The Covenants of Promise*, 63.

It is this covenant relationship and its formative component which legitimates, animates, and ultimately makes for effective reformative discipline. Outside of this relationship, the imposition of discipline would be presumptuous, absent, or likely ineffective. Biblical discipline is only really comprehensible within the context of relationship, the *berith* or covenant that is such a major, if not the primary, theme in the Older Testament.

DISCIPLINE AS THE ACTION OF A LOVING TEACHER[22]

Within the context of the covenant then, in many of the Older Testament passages that speak to the meaning and importance of discipline, God is presented as a teacher whose goal is the welfare of his people, his students as it were: God's disciplinary measures are intended to shape his people so that they live lives of faithfulness and obedience. While God is always motivated by love and always acts with a view to the salvation of his people, divine discipline does, however, entail the punishment of recalcitrant individuals—those who do not ". . . turn, and live" (Ezek 18:32). As noted above, the two Hebrew words in Scripture that are usually translated into Latin as *disciplina* have both formative and reformative connotations.[23] "The [Older Testament] bears witness to God's self revelation to Israel and intervention in his life [i.e., the life of Jacob, renamed Israel]. In response to his love and care for the chosen people, [God] expects trust and obedience in return. The priestly nation is to be stamped with God's nature, and to become increasingly fitted for the sphere of his holiness. The trouble that God has with his people forces Him to severe disciplinary measures, or chastening (*yasar/musar*)."[24]

Whereas the classical Greek approach to such discipline was basically anthropocentric, the Hebrew understanding was theocentric. God himself initiated the process and determined the ends of discipline, always with a view to the salvation of his people. Thus all who truly belong to him should submit gladly to his plan, which is ". . .to lead his people to the realization that they owe their existence to the saving will of Yahweh alone, and therefore owe obedience to their divine instructor . . ."[25] In the

---

22. *The Hebrew/Chaldee Supplement* to *Strong's Exhaustive Concordance to the Bible* and the *Hebrew Aramaic Lexicon of the Old Testament* (*HALOT*) are the sources of much of the information in this section.

23. Brown et al, *Hebrew and English Lexicon of the Old Testament*, 416.

24. Furst, "*Paideuō*," 776.

25. Ibid., 777.

words of Deuteronomy, this divine instructor corrects his people just as parents correct their children (Deut 8:1–6). God's goodness and love are like those of a good parent, who must allow his or her children to suffer, through which experience they will learn that they need "everything that proceeds out of the mouth of the LORD" far more than they need food (Deut 8:3). So too will they learn to trust him, to "keep the commandments of the LORD your God, by walking in his ways and by fearing him" (Deut 8:6). Such divine action is truly an expression of God's love for his people, a love so great that he will correct them, reform them when necessary.[26] Even though, in the Older Testament, God is not often presented as the father of each human being the way Jesus speaks of God as "Abba," there are hints of it and allusions to it, as here in Deuteronomy 8. Indeed, perhaps a shift, a movement toward that understanding may be seen in the Older Testament's treatment of discipline. The God of the Older Testament is often caricatured as an angry, thunderbolt-wielding legalist who demands, and is only interested in, obedience to his demands, and who swiftly punishes those who abrogate the law. That picture runs right up against passages such as the ones under discussion, in which God is portrayed as a teacher wishing to guide his people through both formative and reformative discipline, as well as the passages which liken God's discipline to that exercised by parents over their children. Would a God who is merely a thunderbolt-wielding legalist be interested in reformation, reconciliation, and restoration?

In ancient Israel, children were educated and trained through the deliberate, albeit informal system of parental example, and through the exercise of the father's priesthood in the home. Parents were admonished to inscribe God's words upon their hearts, and to ". . . teach them diligently to your children, and [ ] talk of them when you sit in your house, and when you walk by the way, and when you lie down, and when you rise"(Deut 6:6-7). In the home, children listened and observed, and parents were exhorted to remember and pass on to their children the examples of God's words and acts of discipline in the history of the people Israel (e.g., Deut 11:2, Lev 26). "[T]he young become accustomed to the life of the nation, which stands under the loving discipline of God. Watching and listening, they enter into the inheritance of their forefathers. For he who hears aright will obey."[27] Although the Wisdom litera-

26. Shires and Parker, "Deuteronomy," 387.
27. Furst, "*Paideuō*," 777.

ture may be seen to reflect a "moralizing and humanizing tendency," i.e., wherein the "... aim of education is now wisdom" (Prov 1:1, 8:33),[28] the central focus of these texts remains God and his providential dealings with his people.[29] Similarly, Palestinian Judaism promoted education as that activity intended to "... produce the [person] who lived in obedience to the will of God ..." or to form or inculcate character based on the standard of the Torah.[30] The semantic range of the Hebrew word *musar*, one of the words commonly translated "discipline," includes the following meanings: "reproof, warning, instruction, restraint, check, bond, correction, discipline, doctrine, instruction, rebuke."[31]

In the Deuteronomic context, discipline meted out by the Lord presumes that Israel knows Yahweh "personally," as it were: Israel's past experience was molded by Yahweh's educative influence.[32] God's omnipotence is intimated in these texts in such terms as "greatness," "mighty hand," and "outstretched arm" (Deut 11:2), and God's nature and deeds, when properly understood, seem to elicit reverential fear from his people. Moses too (see Deuteronomy 29) reflected on the value and intent of God's dealings with his people within the confines of the family relationship of the wider faith community of Israel. The community, through its elders, was enjoined and empowered to support the family in imposing discipline on those whose conduct threatened the harmony, holiness, and distinctiveness of both the family and the community. Why? Because Israel's life and prosperity depended upon obedience to Yahweh, who revealed himself as both strong deliverer and stern disciplinarian. Discipline therefore evidently secures and preserves the distinctiveness of God's people, while at the same time it exemplifies God's providence and love: the prodigal who turns and returns (i.e., repents) is welcomed; no hostility is shown to him or her. The ultimate goals of discipline were the preservation of both family heritage and national reputation as well as the deterrence of the spread of evil.

Under the casuistic laws as set out in Deuteronomy (8:5; 21:18–22; 22:18), the principle of obedience to parents is paramount. The child must be respectful of both parents who, in turn, have the support of

28. Ibid., 777.
29. Ibid.
30. Ibid.
31. Blenkinsopp, "Deuteronomy," 109.
32. Ibid., 109.

the community through the elders. If disciplinary measures were to be imposed for sin, the latter made the final decision, seeking to ensure that that they might thus "... get rid of the evil ... brought into the community" (Deut 21:21). When the punishment for a certain sin was death, the community went so far as to expose the corpse of the disobedient one to public view. While surely a revolting idea to modern minds, the rationale was that seeing the body would serve as a warning to others.[33] It is not really very different from the way a wrecked car might be strategically placed near a highway to warn reckless drivers. This principle of admonition through a visible symbol or action is arguably the same as one of the principles underlying excommunication: the community must sometimes make a dramatic statement or take dramatic action to communicate the serious, potentially eternal consequences of the sin of the unrepentant, in the hope that this action may prove a deterrent to others.

This notion of discipline as an expression of parental concern is further reflected in God's persistent provision of instruction designed for the happiness and rest of his people. Likewise, punishment is intended to save them from potentially destructive forces; it is not designed to destroy them (Ps 94:10,12; 118:18). And this picture of God's gracious dealings with his people must be seen in the context of relationship—pre-existing, newly established, or as it is being renewed. The record of the prophet Amos puts this into perspective in Yahweh's declaration: "You only have I known of all the families of the earth; therefore I will punish you for all your iniquities" (Amos 3:2). Discipline is meted out in the context of relationship, a truly intimate family setting ordered by a covenant that binds the human parties who have chosen to subscribe to its demands.

CHASTISEMENT IN THE OLDER TESTAMENT

Although it may come as a surprise to some readers, "chastise," the word used in most traditional English translations of the Scriptures as a translation of *yasar/musar*, does not merely mean "to correct (authoritatively) the faults of; to amend; or to reform."[34] Chastise also embraces

---

33. Ibid., 114.

34. "chastise, verb" *Oxford Dictionary of English*. Edited by Angus Stevenson. Oxford University Press, 2010. Oxford Reference Online. Oxford University Press. Acadia University. 1 April 2011. http://www.oxfordreference.com/views/ENTRY.html?subview=Main&entry=t140.e0139560.

the other aspect of discipline: teaching or formation. This connotation of chastisement is to be found, among other places, in the following passages: Deut 8:1–5—regarding hardship and trials as means of discipline; Deut 22:18–22—correction for consecration; Lev 26:1–20, 40–46—punishment intended to encourage repentance; Ps 94:10,12—chastening as instruction and blessing; Ps 118:18—punishment, but salvation from death; and in the statement in Amos 3:1–8 that discipline is being meted out *because* Israel is the chosen people, the only one among the "families of the earth" that God has known.

The story of Achan, told in Joshua 7, illustrates a number of these principles. In this episode, God disciplines all of Israel for Achan's disobedience, thereby illustrating the destructive and communal nature and effect of sin. Because he kept some of what was, by God's command, supposed to have been "devoted to destruction" (such was the instruction of the *cherem*, the ban), Achan made himself, his family, and the nation unclean and therefore exposed to God's judgment. The crisis vividly shows both the organic nature of community life intended by God for his people—i.e., people are not isolated, individual units—and the vulnerability of the community to sin committed by its individual members. The story also illustrates another important principle of reformative discipline in a covenant relationship: an individual must know and understand the command or prohibition and must voluntarily submit to its authority before he or she can be held accountable for obeying or disobeying it. Here, Achan's own knowledge condemned him, as is revealed in his responses to Joshua's questioning. He knew that the spoils of war were to be destroyed and not used for personal enrichment. The principle to be extracted from this story is that discipline is only legitimately applied where there has been adequate teaching or instruction as well as voluntary commitment to the principle and intent of the command. The following words from Proverbs summarize the issue:

> My son, if you receive my words and treasure up my commandments with you . . . then you will understand the fear of the LORD and find the knowledge of God. For the LORD gives wisdom; from his mouth come knowledge and understanding; he stores up sound wisdom for the upright; he is a shield to those who walk in integrity, guarding the paths of justice and preserving the way of his saints. Then you will understand righteousness and justice and equity, every good path; for wisdom will come into your heart, and knowledge will be pleasant to your soul; discre-

> tion will watch over you; understanding will guard you; delivering you from the way of evil, from men of perverted speech, who forsake the paths of uprightness to walk in the ways of darkness (Prov 2:1, 5–13).

Discipline then is a practice that provides a deterrent to the human propensity to succumb to the pervasiveness and invasiveness of sin and evil and is intended as a protection from their destructive consequences. The story of Achan, as difficult as it can be for readers—especially modern readers—to understand, makes it absolutely clear that the primary purpose of discipline is manifestly not to make people suffer. Nor does it gladden God's heart to punish his people. Rather the purpose is to preserve and make secure a distinct community in faithful relationship to Yahweh, their Lord, their teacher, and their father. Such dramatic consequences of sin may be compared to the practice of excommunication in the Christian community, where deliberate and selfish rebellion against God's moral standards may result in someone's removal from fellowship with the faith community.

The covenant principle as a regulatory factor in the divine-human relationship becomes even clearer in the New Testament (e.g., in Matt 26:26–28; Mark 14:24), as will be seen in the next chapter, although the characterization of the parties to the covenant is different. Indeed, it is only in the establishment of the new covenant that people gain true membership in the "family of God." Under the old covenant, the people were most often described as servants of God; in the new covenant, they have become children, heirs and joint heirs in the family of God (John 1:12; Gal 3:26–27). The discussion of discipline in the New Testament will demonstrate that discipline, exercised regularly and consistently for the formation and reformation of the beloved, namely family members (Heb 12:7–12), is an appropriate and indispensable expression of love, indeed a hallmark of the covenant relationship: ". . . we have had earthly fathers to discipline us and we respected them. Shall we not much more be subject to the Father of spirits and live?" (Heb 12:9).

FOR FURTHER REFLECTION . . .

Meditation

When you call on me, when you come and pray to me, I'll listen. When you come looking for me, you'll find me. Yes, when you get serious about finding me and want it more than anything else, I'll make sure you won't be disappointed." God's Decree. "I'll turn things around for you. I'll bring you back from all the countries into which I drove you"—God's Decree—"bring you home to the place from which I sent you off into exile. You can count on it. (Jer 29:12–14, *The Message*)

Thought

An active prayer life is foundational to being a disciplined disciple. Effective prayer is giving God's work into his hands to accomplish his will.

Questions for Personal and Group Reflection

(1) The word "covenant" refers to an agreement between two or more parties to abide by certain values for the harmony and benefit of the relationship, having each others' best interests at heart. Based on the discussion in the chapter, explain how discipline might be helpful in such a relationship.

(2) Do you believe it is any easier to accept and exercise discipline if it is seen as a safeguard for healthy relationships? Or if it is understood as an act of love? Explain.

(3) According to this chapter, biblical discipline is seen to be directed only at those who have a relationship with God. Do you agree or disagree? Explain your answer on the basis of Scripture.

3

Discipline in the New Testament

The sinfulness endemic to human beings evidently necessitated the institution of a new covenant between the people and God, one ". . . enacted on better promises . . ." than the first, according to the Epistle to the Hebrews (8:6–13). In the following chapter of the epistle, the Older Testament teaching about covenant is connected to the theology of the new covenant in these words: "Therefore he is the mediator of a new covenant, so that those who are called may receive the promised eternal inheritance, since a death has occurred which redeems them from the transgressions under the first covenant" (Heb 9:15). The Greek word *diathēkē*, rendered "covenant" in this passage, is commonly understood as more or less equivalent to the Hebrew word *berith* as used in the Older Testament. In the Septuagint, the Greek translation of the Hebrew Bible produced between two and three hundred years before the birth of Christ, the word *berith* is most often rendered by the Greek *diathēkē*.

The word *diathēkē* refers to a variety of legal and religious relationships, including, of course, God's relationship with humanity; hence it is understood to mean a divinely instituted fellowship involving such elements as "faith" and "religious feelings."[1] The link between the Older Testament people of God and the believers of the New Testament rests on their participation in the common experience of Yahweh's gracious choice to make them his covenant people, a people he describes as ". . . my own possession . . . a kingdom of priests and a holy nation" (Exod 19:5–6), titles that set them apart from other nations. The apostle Peter cites this very passage in reference to the New Testament saints (1 Pet 2:5, 9–11).[2] Notably, both the character and conduct of the elect are stipulated

1. De Koster, "Church Discipline," 238.
2. McComiskey, *The Covenants of Promise*, 69.

in this passage, reiterating God's call upon Israel and now the church to reflect his character in the world. It is furthermore clear that obedience and submission are considered the standards of covenant faithfulness. And just as *berith* entailed both blessings and penalties based on obedience or disobedience, so does *diathēkē* (1 Cor 11:27–32,12:3).

There is, however, a clear difference between the two covenants in the shift from external to internal motivation for obedience. The Older Testament contains hints and echoes of the shape of this covenant to come. Both Jeremiah (31:31–34) and Ezekiel (36:26–27), for example, promulgate the novel principle that loyalty to the covenant with Yahweh requires "a heart of flesh" or a "new heart." Ezekiel emphasizes the importance of the Spirit's presence in the hearts of those in covenant relationship with God, identifying this element as the fundamental difference between the two covenants (Ezek 36:21–38). Isaiah too predicts a new era in which God would captivate and regulate the human heart through the residency of the Holy Spirit (Isa 61:1–11), encouraging obedience to a new covenant and calling forth its blessings, including forgiveness of sins and the Spirit's continuous, indwelling ministry.[3] Again, the major shift pointed to is from external motivation to that arising from the indwelling presence of the Spirit in the believer's life. Jesus himself would later define the heart (*kardia*) as the locus of both obedience and, as is outlined in Mark 7, disobedience—i.e., spiritual pollution of the human being—"all these evil things come from within" (Mark 7:20–23), while the apostle Paul declared that "faith in Christ" was the source and foundation of obedience—i.e., following in his ways—and of blessings in the new covenant (Rom 3:21,22; Gal 3:12).[4] The words of Jeremiah tell plainly the nature of this new spiritual relationship with God and the concomitant new spiritual nature of human beings:

> Behold, the days are coming, says the LORD, when I will make a new covenant with the house of Israel and the house of Judah, not like the covenant which I made with their fathers when I took them by the hand to bring them out of the land of Egypt, my covenant which they broke, though I was their husband, says the LORD. But this is the covenant which I will make with the house of Israel after those days, says the LORD: I will put my law within them, and I will write it upon their hearts; and I will be their God,

---

3. Dumbrell, *Covenant and Creation*, 169.
4. McComiskey, *The Covenants of Promise*, 82.

and they shall be my people. And no longer shall each man teach his neighbor and each his brother, saying, 'Know the LORD,' for they shall all know me, from the least of them to the greatest, says the LORD, for I will forgive their iniquity, and I will remember their sin no more. (Jer 31:31–34)

This new covenant is animated and characterized by several features, including these: (1) the very nature of those who are party to the covenant would be changed; (2) the divine-human relationship would be re-established; (3) participants in the covenant would have a new kind of relationship with God; and (4) God would graciously plan to forget our sins. This new state of the heart secures an inward motivation to obedience;[5] this new relationship is one that ". . . facilitates obedience by the gracious work of God which it expresses and guarantees."[6] In order that his people might keep the covenant, God provided the ministry of the indwelling Holy Spirit to move people from a position of guilt to one of faith and forgiveness—a "forgiveness of sins which was to be so complete that sin would no longer be remembered."[7]

DIATHĒKĒ AS "TESTAMENT" AND "WILL"

The word *diathēkē* is not always rendered "covenant" in English translations of the New Testament; its semantic range is also seen to include "testament" and "will" (the noun), as well as "promise" or "agreement," depending on the context. As the following brief survey of its use in the New Testament illustrates, however, the basic meaning of the word is "a relationship with God," no matter which of these translations is adopted. So, once again, it is to this relational element we turn to understand and appreciate the *diathēkē* as the context for the exercise of discipline in the community of believers in Christ.

The word *diathēkē* appears more often in the Epistle to the Hebrews than in any other book of the New Testament. In certain places—notably in chapter 9:16–17—it is commonly translated "last will and testament," whereas in the Pauline Epistles and in the Gospels it is most often translated "covenant," a rendering deriving its theological significance from

---

5. Ibid., 84–85.
6. Ibid., 92.
7. Dumbrell, *Covenant and Creation*, 200.

its appearance in the accounts of the Last Supper.[8] Both nuances, "covenant" and "last will and testament," find expression in the teachings of Jesus Christ and the apostle Paul and establish a clear link between the Older and the New Testaments, a link sometimes characterized as one of prophecy and fulfillment: "In both form and content the New Testament use of *Diathēkē* follows that of the Old Testament. The only difference is to be found in the step from prophecy to fulfillment . . . *Diathēkē* is from first to last the "disposition" of God, the mighty declaration of the sovereign will of God in history, by which He orders the relation between Himself and men according to His own saving purpose, and which carries with it the authoritative divine ordering, the one order of things which is in accordance with it."[9] The covenant in both Testaments is the relationship initiated by Yahweh, who then both secures and regulates it. Furthermore, the New Testament's *diathēkē* provides for ". . . a binding order of things established by God and based on forgiveness of sins . . ." to enable the establishment of a community that reflects the characteristics of love and obedience.[10]

The word *diathēkē* appears a mere thirty-three times in the New Testament (*berith* occurs 289 times in the Older Testament); nevertheless, its doctrinal meaning is clear. When Jesus introduces the Lord's Supper, it is as a commemoration of the new *diathēkē* (Matt 26:28; Mark 14:24; Luke 22:20; cf. Paul's writing in 1 Cor 11:25), with the terms "new" and "blood of the covenant" pointing back to the Older Testament (Exod 24:5–8; Jer 31:34). The Last Supper, the *seder* or Jewish covenant meal, was subsequently subsumed within the Christian communion rite (1 Cor 10:16–17; Acts 2:46).

Jesus' actions at the Passover meal imbued the ordinary elements of bread and wine—common to the *seder* meal throughout the Older Testament and in his day (Exod 12:15; 13:3,7; Deut 16:3)—with new meaning, and provided another link between the Testaments. His actions also revealed his self-understanding as Messiah, the Lamb of God (Isa 51:13–53:12; John 1:29, John 10), whose ministry fulfilled prophecy (Exod 24:8; Zech 9:11; Jer 31:31–34).[11]

---

8. *Diathēkē, Exegetical Dictionary of the New Testament*, 299–301.

9. Behm and Quelle, "*Diathēkē*," 134.

10. Hillers, *Covenant*, 182,186.

11. Carson, "Matthew," 536–37. Furthermore, Wessel links *diathēkē* with *berith* and concludes that God established a relationship with humanity based on the death of

The apostle Paul regarded the *diathēkē* as the perfect manifestation of Yahweh's grace to his people, visibly demonstrated in the Last Supper and fully realized in Christ's life, death, and resurrection. God's self-giving in Christ is intended to elicit the proper response of a similar self-giving of believers in a relationship of trust and obedience. One commentator has written that through this divine initiative, "God gives Himself to [man and man] gives himself to God for that full measure of mutual acquaintance and enjoyment of which each side is capable."[12] Others concur that the institution of the covenant exemplifies the gift of grace for human redemption through faith (Gal 3:6–9; 4:4–7): Grace takes the form of a new, irrevocable[13] and permanent[14] covenant. In choosing to use the word *diathēkē*, the author of Hebrews is arguably seeking to suggest the breadth of the semantic range and rich associations of the word with both the sovereignty of God and the nature of the covenant.[15] Moreover, its use also avoids negating the importance of the first covenant—indeed that first covenant is now re-established and fulfilled in the redemptive work of Christ: "Think not that I have come to abolish the law and the prophets; I have come not to abolish them but to fulfill them" (Matt 5:17).[16] Some commentators, based on their interpretation of Paul's understanding (Gal 3:15–17), agree that the word carries both connotations. Others disagree; yet they affirm the link between the context of its use in Hebrews with the Older Testament covenant teachings that required a death for its ratification.[17] In the end, the context for the Older and New Testament covenants is relationship, founded by virtue of the divine initiative. Thus, the "inheritance" that accrues to the heirs of the new covenant is ". . . a covenant graciously bestowed by God upon His people, by which He brings them into a special relationship

---

Christ—"the blood of the covenant." Wessel, "Mark," 761.

12. Vos, "Hebrews," 622, 624.
13. Ghurt, "*Diathēkē*," 365.
14. Hughes, *A Commentary on the Epistle to the Hebrews*, 365–66.
15. Vos, "Hebrews," 624.
16. Ibid., 624.
17. Westcott, *Epistle to the Hebrews*, 304. It is argued that the sacrificial death of Christ satisfies the demands of both covenant and testament while simultaneously affirming that "God is the sole author of the covenant which he appoints for his people, while their obedience to its terms is required if they are to enjoy its benefits." Hughes, *A Commentary on the Epistle to the Hebrews*, 369.

with Himself."[18] Such an act of grace allows Christ to be "testator and executor in one, surety and mediator alike,"[19] an identity that supports both the testamentary and covenantal implications of *diathēkē*. A death opens the way for someone to receive an inheritance. In Christ's case, death and resurrection accomplished both, i.e., forgiveness of sin and eternal life, making it possible for God's family by faith to receive the inheritance as heirs and joint heirs. The author of Hebrews arguably emphasizes the need for a third party whose life (and shed blood) played a mediatorial role in the establishment of a relationship with God, Christ, of course, being that "third party" through whom an eternal relationship with God and humanity became a reality.

When those brought into this new relationship commit sin, it affects the new covenant, both individually and corporately, and some form of redress is required to effect its repair and restoration. In Israel, observance of the Day of Atonement as well as acts of individual penitence were part of this effort; it remains to be seen what form such redress is to take under the new *diathēkē*, the new covenant.[20]

DISCIPLINE IN THE NEW TESTAMENT

The New Testament appears to propound a fourfold definition of "discipline": (1) an ecclesiastical function related to the formative discipline commanded in the Great Commission, i.e., "teach them to observe all things" (Matt 28:19–20); (2) a practice requiring the disciples' voluntary submission to the discipline of a master, as a learner preparing to do the master's will; (3) becoming knowledgeable about that will as revealed through preaching and teaching (Matt 16:19; 18:18); and (4) supervision of the disciples' behavior to encourage obedience and the formation of a life of good works. This final definition may also be seen to incorporate

---

18. Bruce, *The Epistle to the Hebrews*, 210.

19. Ibid., 213. In his commentary, R. McL.Wilson propounds that, barring the attendant difficulties of the text, the significant point being made by the writer of Hebrews is that it is ". . . the conviction of the saving power of the death of Jesus that controls the argument, rather than any considerations of logic." Nonetheless, it is acknowledged that the writer displays an informed understanding of the necessity of a new covenant based on Older Testament typology. *The New Century Bible Commentary: Hebrews*, 158.

20. Neil, *The Epistle to the Hebrews*, 96, 98. Also, the allusions to cultic rituals and priestly consecrations of the Old Covenant (Heb 9:17–19) respecting purifications are declared to be ". . . a conflation of practices that were superficial, though provisional, now replaced by a better system." Attridge, *The Epistle to the Hebrews*, 256, 257.

the theme of admonition, i.e., corrective or reformative discipline,[21] as can be seen in Jesus' rebuke of Peter following Jesus' prediction of his death (Matt 16:21-28; 17:22,23) and in Jesus' correction of the disciples' misunderstanding of greatness in the kingdom (Matt 18:1-5; 20:20-28; cf. Mark 10:35-45.)

In the New Testament, it is the Greek noun *paideia* and its verbal cognate, *paideuō,* which are usually translated in English as nominal or verbal forms of the words discipline, teaching, instruction, correction, or chastisement. The semantic ranges of *paideia* and *paideuō* are thus clearly understood to include both formation (teaching, instruction) and reformation (correction, chastisement), divine actions intended ". . . to make (believers) share the very holiness of God Himself."[22] The noun *paideia* may be understood as the function which "regulates character" through "instruction and nurture," or as a "divinely ordained process" which may include teaching and reprimand.[23] Discipline—including reformative discipline—is thus a positive phenomenon, intended to move believers toward a greater understanding of the consequences of sin, and to instill in them an appropriate fear of God's judgment, motivating offenders toward repentance and restoration from guilt due to sin.[24]

The verb *paideuō* is likewise defined as "to practice discipline," "to provide instruction for informed and responsible living," "to assist in the development of a person's ability to make appropriate choices." Its formative and reformative senses can be seen in a large number of passages—for example, Luke 23:16,22; Acts 7:22; 22:3 (instruction and teaching); 1 Cor 11:32 (suffering as discipline); 2 Cor 6:9 (suffering as discipline); 1 Tim 1:20; 2 Tim 2:25 (instruct, teach); Titus 2:12 (instruct, teach); Heb 12:7,10 (Older Testament link); and Rev 3:19 (punish).

THE EXAMPLE OF ANNANIAS AND SAPPHIRA

In terms of the reformative aspect of discipline, the account of Annanias and Sapphira in Acts 5 seems to be the closest New Testament parallel to the Older Testament story of Achan (Joshua 7), i.e., an account of

21. So argues Jeffrey Gibbs, *Concordia Commentary: Matthew 11:2-20:34,* 888.
22. Stibbs, "*Paideia,*" 1214.
23. *Exegetical Dictionary of the New Testament,* Vol. 1, 299-30.
24. Nicoll, *The Expositor's Greek New Testament,* Vol. 2, 367. Other writers refer to this formative aspect of discipline as "intellectual and moral" training. See, e.g., Moulton and Milligan, *The Vocabulary of the Greek Testament,* 473-74.

divine discipline applied at a strategic point in the religious community. Evidently colluding to deceive the apostles about a business transaction and a benevolent offering, the couple brazenly lied, disobeying covenant stipulations regarding truthfulness. Death was the swift and sure punishment for this act, Luke tells us, as it was in the case of Achan, and it offered an example to the fledging congregation of God's discipline and design for holiness. It is important that we understand this situation in terms of the larger covenant community and not simply in terms of the individuals involved. Corrective discipline was necessary where self-discipline had failed, thus serving to remind the members of the covenant community of their responsibility to obey. Discipline is a "faith family" issue, and genuine children of God willingly submit themselves to it or risk being regarded as illegitimate children.[25] God's purpose in exercising discipline is to express his concern about his children's relationship with him. This is God ". . . portrayed as Father who reaches out to His children in order to preserve them in a relationship of love, peace and holiness."[26]

> And have you forgotten the exhortation which addresses you as sons?—"My son, do not regard lightly the discipline of the Lord, nor lose courage when you are punished by him. For the Lord disciplines him whom he loves, and chastises every son whom he receives." It is for discipline that you have to endure. God is treating you as sons; for what son is there whom his father does not discipline? If you are left without discipline, in which all have participated, then you are illegitimate children and not sons. Besides this, we have had earthly fathers to discipline us and we respected them. Shall we not much more be subject to the Father of spirits and live? For they disciplined us for a short time at their pleasure, but he disciplines us for our good, that we may share his holiness. For the moment all discipline seems painful rather than pleasant; later it yields the peaceful fruit of righteousness to those who have been trained by it. (Heb 12:5–11)

Biblical discipline thus involves both instruction and punishment, lovingly directed to members of God's family and intended to serve our best interests. Instruction, or formative discipline, is designed to elicit obedience that results in blessings and divine favor for those committed to living within its parameters. Correction and punishment are the re-formative elements of discipline, applied in order to restore the penitent

---

25. Nicoll, *The Expositor's Greek New Testament*, 367.
26. Furst, "*Paideuō*," 776.

who has transgressed. Those who respond willingly to this ministry of pastoral or soul-care readily acknowledge the assaults of Satan in their lives, their sins, and their consequent exposure to the righteous judgment and just punishment of God. They also submit to the love—and, through confession and repentance—seek the forgiveness as well as the restorative ministry of the fellowship of faith to which they belong.

As in the Older Testament, the notion of discipline having a twofold nature—formation and reformation, admonition and punishment—is maintained in the New Testament, through stories related to teaching and chastening in the training of children (e.g., Acts 22:3; 1 Tim 1:20; Titus 2:12). The word *paideia* is also used in reference to one who has an intense professional involvement with children,[27] a connection that strengthens the notion of discipline as a practice exercised in the context of a relationship between God and his children (as described in John 1:12; 3:3, 5 and Heb 12:9, 10).[28] In some instances of the use of *paideia* or *paideuō* in the New Testament, human action is indicated (2 Tim 2:25; Heb 12:7,10), while in others divine initiation and action is described (1 Cor 11:32; 2 Cor 6:9; Heb 12:6,10; Rev 3:19), especially where Satan is seen to be an instrument of salutary discipline (1 Cor 5:4–5; 1 Tim 1:20).[29] The primary meaning of *paideia*, "the act of providing guidance for responsible living,"[30] also includes the element of correction and punishment,[31] for both formation and reformation are intended to produce godly character in God's children. And that reformation may include suffering, which can, when it is motivated by love, produce positive effects (Rev 1:5; 3:9, 19) for the benefit of the believer (1 Cor 11:32; 2 Cor 4:17; 12:7).[32] Divine love sustains and safeguards the beloved, even to the point of inflicting wounds. Perhaps the cases of Achan and his family, as well as that of Annanias and Sapphira, must be regarded as symbolic of the most extreme excommunication—there is no indication of hope for restoration in either story—and this fact must be considered in contrast to Jesus' admonition to forgive seventy times seven, surely implying, as will be discussed later, the requirement that ongoing efforts

---

27. Bertram, "*Paideia*," 596.
28. Morris, "*Hebrews*," 137.
29. Bauer, "*Paideia*," 603–4.
30. Ibid., through Accordance.
31. Liddell and Scott, *A Greek-English Lexicon*, 1107.
32. Oepke, "Sickness and Sin" and "The Church and Sickness," 1094–98.

should be made to invite and encourage restoration, the seeking of the "one lost sheep." The effort and intent of discipline is always to encourage a return to loyalty and restoration of the relationship.[33]

In the New Testament, therefore, discipline clearly has two aspects. First and foremost, it is formative: discipline is designed to instruct as well as to elicit obedience and bestow blessings. The second, reformative aspect is the effort directed to the restoration of those who have transgressed the parameters of the relationship, those who deserve divine punishment but who, if earnestly penitent, may be restored to the fellowship ruptured by sin.

It is also clear from the New Testament that *agapē*, the unconditional love of God, is the ultimate—and the only valid—motive and method for attempting this vital ministry in an age when right seems wrong, and wrong seems right, and in which everyone does what is right in his or her own eyes. As in the Older Testament, this love, this *agapē*, finds its authority and effective outworking within the context of the divine-human relationship, the *berith*, the *diathēkē*, the covenant. In the Older Testament, this point was made in Yahweh's affirmation to Israel: "You have I known above all the families of the earth, therefore I will punish you for all your iniquities" (Amos 3:2). In the New Testament, the first epistle of Peter (2:4–10) parallels Amos' admonition, reiterating the principle that God disciplines because of the family relationship established through the covenant.

How then might one approach the act of exercising Christian discipline? What principles—consistent with life in community—and what processes might best be employed in order to foster and secure the faithfulness of the community and its members to the truth and intent of Scripture? These concerns shall be considered in the chapters to come.

FOR FURTHER REFLECTION . . .

Meditation

> In this all-out match against sin, others have suffered far worse than you, to say nothing of what Jesus went through—all that bloodshed! So don't feel sorry for yourselves. Or have you forgotten how good parents treat children, and that God regards you as his children?

---

33. Nicoll, *The Expositor's Greek New Testament*, 372.

My dear child, don't shrug off God's discipline, but don't be crushed by it either. It's the child he loves that he disciplines; the child he embraces, he also corrects. God is educating you; that's why you must never drop out. He's treating you as dear children. This trouble you're in isn't punishment; it's training, the normal experience of children. Only irresponsible parents leave children to fend for themselves. Would you prefer an irresponsible God? We respect our own parents for training and not spoiling us, so why not embrace God's training so we can truly live? While we were children, our parents did what seemed best to them. But God is doing what is best for us, training us to live God's holy best. At the time, discipline isn't much fun. It always feels like it's going against the grain. Later, of course, it pays off handsomely, for it's the well-trained who find themselves mature in their relationship with God.

So don't sit around on your hands! No more dragging your feet! Clear the path for long-distance runners so no one will trip and fall, so no one will step in a hole and sprain an ankle. Help each other out. And run for it! (Heb 12:4–13, *The Message*)

Thought

Prayer that is based on relationship and not transaction may be the most freedom-enhancing way of connecting to a God whose vantage point we can never achieve and can hardly imagine.[34]

Questions for Personal and Group Reflection

(1) The New Testament presumes that discipline is a "family matter," practiced among those related to God and each other through a covenant. Explain your understanding of this covenant: how did it come into being and upon what basis was it established? How do people become partners in it?

(2) Compare and contrast the experiences of discipline of Achan (Josh 7) and Annanias and Sapphira (Acts 5). How are they similar? How are they different? Do you believe the discipline applied was too extreme? Why? How do the principles underlying the discipline imposed in these passages relate to those outlined in 1 Corinthians 5 and 10?

Are these principles relevant to Christian living today?

---

34. Yancey, *Prayer: Does It Make Any Difference?*, 55.

4

Christian Discipline: Views from the Congregation

Having outlined the fundamental biblical context—the covenant relationship between God and his people—the warrant of authority, and the call for the practice of discipline, formative and reformative, we turn now to possible explanations for its decline. The comments of respondents to a survey on Christian discipline of members of several local congregations fairly reflect, it is suggested, the range and diversity of views held by many in the community of believers.

Whereas church discipline used to be seen as one of the ". . . marks by which the true church is known,"[1] a church in our day which imposes significant disciplinary measures is often, if incorrectly, cast in a negative light. Indeed, the imposition of discipline may even be seen as ". . . the mark of a false church, bringing to mind images of witch trials, scarlet letters, public humiliations, and damning excommunications."[2] Indeed, the term "Christian discipline" rather than "church discipline" is being deliberately used in this book because of the negative connotations and associations of the latter, some of which, it must be admitted, arise from very real abuses of church discipline over the centuries.

POSSIBLE FACTORS IN THE DECLINE OF DISCIPLINE

Several factors might be cited for the decline, or in some cases the demise, of discipline in the church. Some blame the revivalist tradition for allegedly encouraging unregenerate church membership. Some point to

---

1. Jeschke, "How Discipline Died." The other two marks were "the preaching of the pure doctrine of the gospel" and the "pure administration of the sacraments."

2. Editor's Introduction to articles on Christian Discipline, *Christianity Today*, 2005.

the current phenomenon of mega-churches, featuring multiple services attracting itinerant, church-hopping, "visitor" worshipers. The suggestion is that such churches may also attract or, in effect, "produce" people likely to avoid, subvert, or escape accountability because there is little or no intentional, ongoing fellowship. Even if pastoral oversight is difficult in some of these fellowships, it must nevertheless be argued that it is still possible to create relationships of mutual care—for example, by intentionally organizing the congregation into small-group ministries, whose nature and size may permit and even facilitate effective discipline and member care.[3] Many small congregations may also be innocent victims/hosts of "Spring to Fall" fever, the phenomenon that occurs when people move out to their cottages or camps for the summer. Churches often see increased attendance and offerings over this period, but the exercise of discipline may be quite limited, if it occurs at all, because people may not feel they are organically connected to the congregation, the locus of accountability.

DISCIPLINE AND LEGALISM

While the demographic shifts described above may account for some of the decline, it has to be acknowledged that a number of serious charges are often made about deficiencies in or problems with the imposition or exercise of discipline, including a lack of clear and deliberate accountability for its implementation, as well as inconsistent disciplinary practices following on inconsistent discipleship and membership strategies. Still more important than these, perhaps, is the fact that many people see church discipline as sheer legalism, i.e., an emphasis on strict conformity to law rather than to spirit, or to the letter of the law rather than to its spirit. The historic roots of this charge may be seen, in part, in the story of the reformed church in Calvin's Geneva, which conceded its responsibility for community discipline to the state. The secular authorities, not the leaders of the Genevan church, dealt with unchristian conduct as well as criminal behavior, leading to a conflation of church discipline and secular law in the minds of many people. The residue of this can still be seen today in the approach of some churches to internal discipline. Ironically, as a consequence of its action, the Genevan church was accused by some of having *abdicated* its spiritual duties with respect to discipline. It is an interesting and telling footnote to this story that some erring Christians actually preferred to be

---

3. Jeschke, "How Discipline Died."

subject to penalties imposed by civil laws and courts rather than accept the grace of accountability for righteousness cultivated through a personal and communal response to sin.[4]

In any case, as Marlin Jeschke points out, the charge of legalism is often substantiated by the reality of "... the church's copying of the state's pattern of dealing with offenders through legalistic machinery: filing charges, setting up courts, holding trials—in short, engaging in casuistry that obscures the spirit of the gospel."[5] In order to restore respect and support for discipline, he urges the church to re-establish Christ's model of discipleship as the foundation and standard for dealing appropriately and effectively with unbecoming conduct of church members.[6]

Although some may argue that the Genevan church compromised with cultural norms when it turned such matters over to the state, we should not lose sight of the fact that its efforts were impelled by its zeal for righteousness, its concern for the life and conduct of saints who could then infiltrate and act upon their society as spiritual catalysts—"truly salt and light"—of the kingdom of God. Unfortunately, the church in this twenty-first century generally not only lacks such zeal, but *is* arguably even less than "lukewarm," more often resembling the world than being radically different from it. Christian discipline should also be about the business of changing this reality, for its formative goal is to nurture the life of purity and to cultivate in believers both a passionate love for God and an ardent desire to be the "image of God" in the world, as directed in Scripture.

DISCIPLINE: MIXED VIEWS

Throughout the history of the church, many efforts have been made to evaluate the effectiveness of discipline and its impact on the health and growth of the local congregation. Results have often been quite mixed. For example, one recent survey of the practice of "strictness"—a synonym for discipline—in two Protestant congregations sought to determine how the practice affected church growth, i.e., whether greater strictness stimulated new membership, and whether the level of discipline practiced or ignored were matters of concern to the average member. Respondents indicated that they believed discipline was a reason that some avoided,

---

4. Ibid.
5. Ibid.
6. Ibid.

but that others affiliated with, certain churches. Interviewees expressed concern for, and appreciation of, certain types of moral and ethical behavior and deportment as determinants of their decisions to associate with a given church, but they also identified such things as ". . . feeling the presence of the Holy Spirit, the family-like nature of congregational life, and the qualities of the pastor"[7] as the major factors behind their decisions to seek membership. This response is interesting because these latter characteristics are not separate from, but are rather reflections of, the formative impact of Christian discipline, hallmarks of a caring and supportive community life in which members are accountable to one another. Such a foundation fosters genuine covenant love that motivates the practice of corrective and reformative discipline (Matt 18; Gal 6:1–10) necessary for discipleship and growth in spiritual maturity. The gospel's promise is that this faithfulness will result in some measure of growth, as the Spirit draws people (Matt 16:18; Eph 4) into the family of faith.

EXPLORING VIEWS ON DISCIPLINE—COMMENTS OF SURVEY RESPONDENTS IN ATLANTIC CANADA

As noted in the Preface, this book is based in part on research completed for a Doctor of Ministry (DMin) dissertation. Members of a number of Baptist congregations in Atlantic Canada were surveyed about their understanding of and support for (or lack thereof) the practice of Christian discipline as an essential facet of the church's ministry, one that marks the church as having a unique and distinctive existence in the world. Asked whether they believe that ". . . the Bible is the inspired word of God, the authority in matters of faith and practice," the majority of respondents said they did. There was significant interest in and earnest general agreement that discipline should be practiced in the church, *if* it could be demonstrated to be both biblically warranted and a productive aspect of the process of discipleship. At the same time, opinions ranged widely as to the specific reformative disciplinary measures churches should implement. One interesting finding was that younger respondents were more supportive of the imposition of disciplinary actions in the church than were those aged sixty-five and over.

---

7. Tamney, "Does Strictness Explain the Appeal of Working-Class Conservative Protestant Congregations?," 283–302.

Representative of the range received are these paraphrased comments:

—I am in full support of Christian discipline where it is biblically sound and compassionately exercised.

—I reject "cut-and-dried" discipline because the uniqueness of each person makes it difficult to do this.

—If we discipline members, they may stay away from the church. On the other hand, if we pray for and love them, they may in time hear God's admonition and repent of all sin.

—I think any sin which the individual is unwilling to deal with should be addressed through Christian discipline. Sin is serious business and we need to seek to follow the biblical approach to discipline, which focuses on the attitude of the sinner rather than the sin.

—If there is no repentance, all sins must be addressed through the exercise of discipline.

—Unaddressed sin has a negative impact on the church's witness in the community, since even the world has certain standards.

—If someone rejects correction and continues in sin, discipline should be imposed.

—If discipline is going to be applied, it has to be done fairly and applied equally to all. There should be no favoritism, regardless of the status of the person involved.

—I'm concerned that the church should not fasten on to certain sins while ignoring others that seem to have become more acceptable.

—If disciplinary measures are going to be imposed, members need to have been taught beforehand what is acceptable conduct in the Christian community. There should not be reformative discipline, in other words, if there hasn't been formative discipline. The whole point of Christ's teaching was to bring sinners to saving grace (salvation) through Christ Jesus. Some people don't know or realize that they are committing sin, and the church needs to point these things out first, offer guidance, counsel, love, and only if all has failed and there is a complete lack of responsibility or care on the individual's part should membership be removed.

—We are all sinners, so I personally do not feel worthy of passing judgment on other members.

—I think discipline should extend to maintaining doctrinal purity, and that there are organizations Christians shouldn't belong to because they are inconsistent with the faith.

—Admonition has to come before discipline.

—This area is often neglected in our churches today. In my recent experience, many people (Christians) wish to ignore this area for fear of offending. This stifles the work of God in our lives and consequently in our churches and communities.

—Prayer, not excommunication, is the proper response to sin: excommunication is completely judgmental. The church is to assist us in becoming more Christ-like and should not be judgmental. Even though we would like to be like him, we are always striving for that ideal, so we should be very careful before we exercise any discipline of others and pray for them instead.

—I'm concerned about how discipline is offered or exercised and how it is received by those to whom it is directed.

—I believe and always have that if we could try our best to follow the Golden Rule, we would have fewer problems both in the church and outside. It is very easy to criticize the other person, but if we go back to the Bible we will find that Jesus said, "Let him who is without sin cast the first stone." In order to help an individual we must not turn them away from the church but as a body of believers and Christ's followers we must try to lend them a helping hand.

—Prayer is extremely important in discipline, as "more things are wrought by prayer than this old world dreams of." I understand the principle, but I don't entirely agree that discipline is the best way to "win back the individual."

—Christian discipline is narrow and un-Christlike. Some things are treated as more serious than others—e.g., adultery versus gossip or discrimination based on color, speech, levels of wealth, age, disabilities (especially mental).

—Any serious attempts at practicing discipline would likely result in reduced membership in churches and would put pastors out of work.

—The most important question to ask is "What would Jesus do?"

—Think about the parables of the lost sheep, the lost coin, and the prodigal son. Though discipline may be necessary at times, it should be done in the spirit of love and kindness . . . it is wrong to excommunicate members since God loves the sinner but hates the sin. He alone has the authority to judge. Since Jesus is the Bread of Life, turning people away would leave them with no recourse to this Bread.

—Discipline in "today's church"—as opposed to a cult—would be ineffective, since people would simply get new friends who accept their lifestyle, and they would turn around and blame the church for turning them away.

—Discipline could be potentially discouraging to the unconverted. I was allowed to provide leadership in a congregation, even though unconverted at the time, and often inebriated when I arrived at church to fulfill my duties. If the church leaders had turned me away or hindered my involvement, I might never have become a Christian.

—I don't think anyone should be kept away from the church. All people deserve God's love; only he knows what is in their hearts. We are to pray for the sinners of this world and not judge their sins; only God can do that.

—All of the inspired word of God must be preached faithfully. I am concerned that the whole counsel of God—the inspired word of God—be preached faithfully in order to address the need for repentance and holy living.

—Offerings are low as it is; it is sometimes difficult to pay a pastor's salary—disciplinary actions would make that more of a problem.

—People are not willing to accept criticism or be accountable before God and others. Corrective discipline is "forced accountability."

—I believe that in most churches, if we were to live truly as God instructs us to, and the minister were to preach and teach God's word as it is written, then church attendance would be very small.

The range of reformative disciplinary actions listed in the survey included personal admonition, suspension from communion, public admonishment (either in a duly called business meeting or in some other forum—e.g., a meeting after a church service—in which only members participate), suspension from church duties, and excommunication. As noted above, opinions ranged widely among respondents in terms of the kinds of reformative disciplinary measures churches should take. Nevertheless, despite some hesitancy, most respondents affirmed that such measures were sometimes required of the church, although opinions were decidedly mixed as to whether Scripture provided clear, explicit directions about their nature and administration. In addition, as noted above, older respondents were less supportive than were younger respondents of more extreme reformative disciplinary measures; in addition, more women than men took that same position. Those people who had been members of the church for longer periods of time (over twenty years in many cases) were likewise less likely to support drastic disciplinary measures, even if they believed there was biblical support for doing so. Those who were more involved in the church—particularly in Bible studies and Sunday School—were more likely to support disciplinary measures, as were those who attended services virtually every week, those who made significant monetary donations to the church, those whose devotional life included daily prayer and study of the Scriptures, and those with higher levels of education. Respondents whose churches had explicit, written covenant documents were also more likely to support reformative disciplinary measures.

Personal admonition of the individual in an effort to, and as the means of, prompting repentance, restoration, and forgiveness from God and the congregation was seen as biblically authorized and appropriate by a significant proportion of respondents, with opinions varying as to whether such admonition should come from the pastor alone or from the deacons and pastor together, or other members of the congregation who were knowledgeable about the issues at hand.

On the other hand, only a small majority of respondents agreed that rejection of the admonition by the church should result in a loss of church privileges and responsibilities, although, curiously, a high percentage of respondents nevertheless agreed that excommunication might be necessary if the erring member completely rejected admonitory efforts, and if the respondents could be shown that such an action was consistent with Scripture. At the same time, there was serious concern about such a drastic move: Some felt that it is an outdated concept; some felt it would adversely affect the church's public reputation; some felt that the prerogative for such an action is God's alone; some argued about whether such an action would infringe an individual's legal rights; many were concerned that such an act would create conflict in the church.

COMMENTARY ON SURVEY RESPONSES

The comments noted above include a number of sound principles, first among them that formation must precede reformation. It is a serious problem for the church to institute reformative disciplinary measures without first having provided positive teaching about what is expected of the community of believers. The attitude of the church toward discipline and the manner in which it is exercised are also important: Does the community exercise discipline with an attitude of loving care in confrontation, both challenging members to lead a holy life and supporting them in that effort? Or is discipline meted out in an atmosphere of self-righteousness and condemnation?

It is however problematic that while a large majority (approximately 70 percent) of respondents asserted their belief that individual sin affects others, nevertheless the comments of many suggested that a person's behavior is a purely personal matter—arguably a contradictory, individualistic position that implicitly denies the corporate effects of sin, as well as the very nature of the church, the covenant that binds believers together and makes the members of the body of Christ accountable one to another. That same individualism might be discerned in the comments of those whose opinion appeared to be based *only* on the potential response to discipline of the individual in question, as well as in the assertion by some that Christian discipline is wholly inappropriate—that it is not for the members of the community to confront one another regarding sinful conduct or to judge one another. That people may choose to "find other friends who will be supportive of their lifestyle" is another troubling comment: is the church then no more than some kind of social gathering? Sadly, too, this view either underestimates or overlooks altogether the possibility of regeneration and its moral impact on the community as well as on individuals.

While it is impossible to know what sort of formation and teaching in the Scriptures respondents received, a significant degree of biblical illiteracy was evident in the patchwork of Bible verses offered by one respondent who rejected discipline as a valid ministry (as in the comment "Christians have no business judging one another; it is a trespass on divine jurisdiction"), as well as in the often sketchy and incomplete picture of biblical evidence proffered in support of it. On the other hand, some support for, and a significant number of the arguments against, the exercise of Christian discipline seemed to be based not on the tenets of the Bible, but rather those of modern humanism.

The results of this survey, while mixed, nevertheless reveal a basic conviction that the church should be a disciplined community of faith, living according to standards and practices that distinguish it from the secular world. While varying significantly in terms of the when, where, who, what, and how, respondents did basically agree that Christian discipline is the appropriate and biblical response to prevent and correct breaches of these standards.

There is no question, however, but that the context in which the church finds itself has always had and continues to have a significant impact on it. "A congregation—its theology and ethics, its worship, its style of operation, and what it does, or does not do with reference to mission—is profoundly shaped by its social context."[8] This statement, which most readers would likely agree is a simple statement of fact, has significant implications about many church matters, not least those related to Christian discipline. How is the church to express its distinct presence in the world, to share its values, and to make an impact? Jesus described his disciples as being "in the world but not of the world." At the same time, the church was given the mandate to evangelize the world: "Go . . . into all the world . . . and make disciples."(Matt 28:19–20) Can Christian congregations, through commitment to and application of both formative and reformative Christian discipline, be catalysts that stimulate change not only internally, but in the larger social context as well, seeking to resist, transcend, and ultimately overcome negative and evil influences through Christ-like love? The bottom line is that the church either shapes its context or is at risk of being shaped by it.

---

8. Carrol, *Handbook of Congregational Studies*, 48.

FOR FURTHER REFLECTION . . .

Meditation

When a woman gives birth, she has a hard time, there's no getting around it. But when the baby is born, there is joy in the birth. This new life in the world wipes out memory of the pain. The sadness you have right now is similar to that pain, but the coming joy is also similar. When I see you again, you'll be full of joy, and it will be a joy no one can rob from you. You'll no longer be so full of questions.

This is what I want you to do: Ask the Father for whatever is in keeping with the things I've revealed to you. Ask in my name, according to my will, and he'll most certainly give it to you. Your joy will be a river overflowing its banks! (John 16:21–24, *The Message*)

Thought

More things are wrought by prayer than this world dreams of, wherefore let thy voice rise like a fountain for me night and day. For what are men better than sheep or goats . . . if knowing God they lift not hands of prayer for themselves and those that call them friend.[9]

Questions for Personal and Group Reflection

(1) This chapter identified a number of reasons for the decline in the practice of discipline. What are they?

(2) Give an example of legalism. Have you ever experienced it in your involvement in a Christian community or congregation?

(3) Discuss the survey responses that encouraged you and those that did not. What are your current views for or against the practice of Christian discipline?

---

9. Tennyson, *Morte d'Arthur*.

5

Christian Discipline: Lessons from History

DISCIPLINE IN THE EARLY CHURCH

Evidence of disciplinary practices undertaken in early Christian communities can be found in such documents as *The Apostolic Constitutions* (c. AD 252–270), which offers this exhortation:

> When you see the offender in the congregation, you are to take the matter heavily, and to give orders that he be expelled from it. Upon his expulsion, the Deacons are likewise to express their concern, to follow and to find the party, and to detain him for a while without the Church. In a little time they are to come back, and to intercede with you on his behalf . . . as our Savior interceded with His Father for sinners, saying, as we learn from the Gospel, "Father, forgive them; for they know not what they do." Then you shall order him to be brought into the Church; and after having examined whether he be truly penitent, and fit to be readmitted into *full* Communion, you shall direct him to continue in a state of mortification for the space of two, three, five, or seven weeks, according to the nature of the offense; and then, after some proper admonitions, shall dismiss [i.e., forgive] him.[1]

Clearly, the early church took Christian discipline seriously, although it also appears to have begun focusing on the gravity of the sin rather than on the attitude of the sinner as enjoined in Matthew 18. The compassionate tone of this passage suggests, nevertheless, that the earnest desire to restore the erring one appears to modulate the ministers' attitude and approach to the application of discipline.

---

1. Jeschke, *Discipling in the Church*, 127.

CHURCH DISCIPLINE IN CALVIN'S GENEVA

Likewise, during the Reformation period in Europe, discipline was assiduously practiced within the church. As has been noted above, the church in Geneva was particularly noteworthy in this regard, seeing discipline as an expression of communal pastoral care directed at "... protecting the weak and vulnerable, educating the ignorant, and mediating interpersonal conflicts . . . the ministers and elders were conscientious in their efforts to care for the flock that they believed God had entrusted to them."[2]

Disciplinary records of the time reveal that the stated intent of such efforts was the desire to encourage restoration of those guilty of moral and religious sins rather than their removal from fellowship. When this last did occur, the individuals were prohibited from participating in the Eucharist, because of the "... sacramental beliefs, symbols, and culture"[3] associated with it. The intent was to hold the church to the ideal of a common standard of faith and practice.[4]

In the Genevan church, elders were discreetly chosen, as were ministers, who were strategically placed so that they could provide adequate oversight of congregants, vigilantly keeping an eye out for immoral behavior. Although this may sound draconian and legalistic, it is important to note that it occurred in the context of spiritual formation: "During annual household visitations the pastors and elders examined their flock's understanding of basic Christian doctrine, offered spiritual counsel and fraternal admonition, intervened in marital conflicts, and identified moral offenses requiring further discipline."[5] Information about sinful behavior also came to the attention of the church through accusations, reports, or rumors, and the resulting ecclesiastical investigations aimed "... to correct misbehavior and promote virtuous conduct and right belief." Disciplinary practices were not as overtly intrusive as they might seem to us, looking at them from our overly individualistic Western perspective.[6]

---

2. Manetsch, "Pastoral Care East of Eden," 277.
3. Ibid., 276.
4. Ibid.
5. Ibid., 278.
6. Ibid.

Indeed, the church today could learn and profit from the example of the disciplinary purposes, processes, and penalties of this church. While it must be admitted that the church tended to emphasize the severity of the sin committed rather than the attitude and response of the sinner, nevertheless the spiritual penalties imposed still sought "... genuine repentance and change of life" intended to benefit both the individual and the greater fellowship. Disciplinary measures included the following:

(1) Private sins or minor moral infractions resulted in stern lectures based on Scripture delivered to the sinners by the ministers and elders, along with pastoral advice and warnings about potential consequences of continued misconduct.

(2) For more serious matters, verbal reproof and admonition by the consistory (the regulatory court in Lutheran churches, perhaps equivalent to the Board of Deacons or Elders in some congregations and communities; it was responsible for oversight of the spiritual life of members).

(3) Mandatory confession and reparation before the entire church. Those who had deliberately neglected their spiritual duties (for example, those who had changed their religious affiliation out of a desire for self-preservation from various forms of persecution) were required, upon their return to fellowship, to publicly confess their sin, to ask for the forgiveness of the congregation, and to reaffirm the particular principle they had denied.

(4) Minor excommunication (suspension). When such suspension involved Communion, it was usually motivated by the desire to preserve the purity of the church, protect Christians from the influence of the wicked, and hasten the repentance and restoration of the sinner, as well as to protect the Lord's Table from spiritual defilement.

(5) Major excommunication (complete exclusion from the fellowship).

In the Genevan community, the value of fellowship was paramount in the exercise of discipline; by the same token, tremendous patience was often required in order to see the fruits of disciplinary efforts. In Geneva, one of the interesting features of church discipline, mentioned previously, was the partnership between church and city magistrates in dealing with criminal acts that required civil punishment, and with infractions of Christian standards that required the imposition of religious disciplinary measures. This partnership brought the practices of the church into public view, subjecting them to public scrutiny, and it served as an indirect public witness of the church and possibly an influence on the behavior of Christians and non-Christians alike. There were three potential dimensions to church discipline: spiritual sanctions, social shame, and the possibility of civil punishment, and they ". . . made suspension and excommunication particularly effective pastoral tools for regulating public behavior and restoring sinners to the visible church."[7]

Unfortunately, some individuals chose to accept civil penalties for their conduct but avoided the church's spiritual intervention, thus short-circuiting its disciplinary ministry. In addition, some offenders appeared to be unwilling to repent of their sins and reluctant to submit to participation in the process of restoration, preferring to voluntarily drop out of the church instead. While unfortunate, these examples actually serve to illustrate the truth that real righteousness and adherence to the moral law must be regulated by the heart submissive to the Spirit, rather than by mere allegiance to human regulations, and they suggest that where these spiritual principles of submission and obedience are practiced, in a context of community support and mutual accountability to the biblical standard of conduct, spiritual formation can be sustained. The church's embrace of Calvin's vision for effecting transformation in moral behavior had a positive impact on pastoral care in Geneva:

> When the members of Geneva's consistory disciplined sinners, their primary (stated) concern was not to organize society, nor to enforce moral behavior, nor even to provide social help. Rather . . . the pastors and elders believed that Scripture commanded them, as shepherds of God's flock, to protect the purity of the Lord's Supper while at the same time attending to the spiritual well-being of sinner-saints struggling against the world, the flesh, and the devil . . . The Geneva consistory was more than a morals court devoted simply to punishing aberrant behavior. It was also committed to the spiritual restoration of the sinner, the instruction of the ignorant, as well as the mediation of the ever-present quarrels that threatened families and strained the social fabric of society.[8]

7. Ibid., 285.
8. Ibid., 305–6.

Moreover, the process of pastoral care included very personal interaction and intervention with congregants: "... ministers and elders met with people face-to-face; they addressed them by name; they listened at length to their grievances; they tried to apply the 'medicine' of church discipline to individual circumstances..."[9] at every level, without regard for class, gender, or social and professional status. Such engagement with the people involved much emphasis on religious education that could guide basic living and spiritual formation: "The objective was more than modifying behavior... Even as they sought the purity of Christ's Church, the Genevan pastors endeavored to provide assistance and guidance for the people of God as they struggled with personal sin and plodded along the pilgrim's path of repentance, forgiveness and restoration ... [The pastors were] committed to interjecting biblical standards of belief and behavior into the profound messiness of human life so as to make possible Christian forgiveness and salvation."[10]

CHRISTIAN DISCIPLINE AT OTHER PERIODS OF CHURCH HISTORY

Various forms of discipline were practiced during the Medieval, Reformation, and succeeding eras of church history, and in places other than Geneva. The Heidelberg Catechism of the Reformed Churches in Germany (1546), for example, reflects their belief that the "keys of the kingdom"(Matt 16:19) were "[t]he preaching of the holy gospel, and Christian discipline, or excommunication out of the Christian church; by these two, the kingdom of heaven is opened up to believers, and shut against unbelievers. [John 21:23; Matt. 18:15-18]"[11] The specific relationship of discipline to entrance into the kingdom is further described here:

> [W]hen, according to the command of Christ, those who, under the name of Christians, maintain doctrines or practices inconsistent therewith, and will not, after having been brotherly admonished, renounce their errors and wicked course of life, are complained of to the church, or to those who are thereunto appointed by the church; and if they despair their admonition, are, by them, forbidden the use of the sacraments; whereby they are excluded from the Christian church, and by God Himself from

---

9. Ibid., 307.
10. Ibid., 312, 313.
11. Wray, *Biblical Church Discipline*, 18.

the kingdom of Christ; and when they promise and show real amendment, are again received as members of Christ and His church. [Matt 18:15; 1 Cor 5:12; Matt 18:15-18; Rom 12:7-10; 1 Cor 12:28; 1 Tim 5: 17; 2 Thess 2:14; Matt 18:17; 1 Cor 5:3-5; 2 Cor 2:6-11; Luke 15:18][12]

Similarly, the Westminster Confession of Faith (1646) affirmed belief in, and the value of, Christian discipline, asserting the divine establishment of church leadership for proper government of the body through the establishment and imposition of principles for the conduct of members. The "keys of the kingdom" were interpreted as proffering divine authority for practicing discipline:

> [B]y virtue whereof, they have power, respectively to retain, and remit sins; to shut that kingdom against the impenitent, both by the Word, and censures; and to open it unto penitent sinners, by the ministry of the Gospel; and by absolution from censures, as occasion shall require. Church censures are necessary, for the reclaiming and gaining of offending brethren, for deterring of others from the like offences, for purging out that leaven which might infect the whole lump, for vindicating the honor of Christ, and the holy profession of the gospel, and for preventing the wrath of God, which might justly fall upon the Church, if they should suffer his covenant, and the seals thereof, to be profaned by notorious and obstinate offenders.[13]

CHRISTIAN DISCIPLINE IN NINETEENTH-CENTURY NORTH AMERICA

Closer to our own time are the efforts to practice Christian discipline made in the nineteenth century (c. 1800–1850) by congregations in the Free Church tradition, who were also referred to as American frontier groups. They included Methodists, Baptists, and Presbyterians, in whose midst discipline resurfaced as a covenant responsibility: "No Christian looked upon his behavior as 'nobody's business . . .'. The members of those pioneer congregations felt both free and obliged to watch over

---

12. Ibid., 18, 19.

13. Ibid., 19. The Congregationalists of New England crafted a similar statement during the Cambridge Synod (1646–1648 in Cambridge, Massachusetts); it is notable for its extensive detailing of the process of exercising Christian discipline, particularly the practices of excommunication and restoration.

each other . . . Moreover, at their best, the systems of admonition and correction were intended as means of repentance and reconciliation for the fallen. Their investigations were not just snooping; they were devised to protect and keep from harm."[14]

The records of five frontier churches in Kentucky between 1800 and 1860 provide an illuminating glance at how seriously discipline was taken. The following were among the reasons, listed in church minutes, for exclusion of members:

> [S]tealing, beating one's wife, telling lies, mistreating another person, gambling, cursing, threatening suicide, drinking too much, fighting, living in adultery, being pregnant outside of marriage, striking one's father-in-law, refusing to attend church, dancing, moving from the state without applying for a letter of dismission, bad conduct in a church meeting, refusing to pay a debt, attending a horse race, denying the faith and doctrine of the church, misrepresenting persons in church to the grand jury in the county, violating the rules of the church, playing cards and billiards, taking out a lawsuit against another person, murder, and betting.[15]

A strong sense of life in community appears to have been the driving force behind this commitment to Christian discipline. Unfortunately, in some cases, discipline became either overly legalistic, or abusive, or trivialized, in spite of its positive intent.

AFFIRMATION OF THE VALUE OF CHRISTIAN DISCIPLINE

Another example of the deliberate, considered practice of Christian discipline in the nineteenth century comes from the 1814 records of the local Baptist church in Chester, Nova Scotia. They tell the story of decisions to apply discipline, the reasons for it, the disciplinary actions taken, and the posture of the congregation in relation to them. At one point, the church noted its resolution to ". . . withdraw our fellowship from [X] for total neglect of Covenant engagements, frolicking and dancing, and from [Y] for neglect of Covenant meeting and Communion, praying the Lord to return them to his fold in his own good time and way."[16] The fortuitous result of such disciplinary action is observed in other min-

14. Jeschke, *Discipling in the Church*, 137.
15. Deweese, *A Community of Believers*, 73.
16. Miles, *The History of The Chester Baptist Church*, 5.

utes from that year: "This year closed with the return of a prodigal, who had long been from home, confessing his wrongs and his weaknesses."[17] Other records show the cohesiveness of churches in disciplinary matters across the larger body of associated churches in the region. Participation in the association was an integral part of church fellowship, and matters affecting congregational health were deliberated and discussed corporately at its meetings. The 1815 records report that the Chester church asked the following question of the association of churches: "What is the most proper treatment toward those members in the church who absent themselves from church meetings and Communion, but in other respects walk circumspectly?"[18] Records for 1816 also include notes about disciplinary measures, including exclusion, imposed for ". . . hard drinking, profanity and quarrelsomeness."[19]

But while the records identify what may seem, especially today, harsh penalties for what might be deemed relatively minor misconduct, the records also reveal the presence of the strongest and surest foundation for the effective exercise of discipline: a strong loving, caring fellowship unafraid to hold its members accountable for living a Christian life. Equally important is the fact that, in this community, discipline was a normal part of church life, not something appealed to or imposed only in circumstances of great crisis.

In addition, when the situation in the congregation was found to be deteriorating, something was done about it. A lament in the 1809 record reads: "We found the house so divided that we thought it could not stand. We found gospel discipline decaying and backsliding increasing."[20] Subsequent notes indicate changes in the life of the congregation, and a return to a healthy spiritual atmosphere marked by fasting and prayers, testimonies and praise. In addition, clear connections are seen in the records between biblical preaching and teaching and the reformative practices of discipline. The unity of the fellowship was also reflected in the opportunities members created to share struggles and temptations and, where necessary, to repent and openly seek forgiveness and restoration. Here is an excerpt from the record itself:

17. Ibid., 5.
18. Ibid., 6.
19. Ibid., 6.
20. Ibid., 3.

The first Saturday in the month of November was a day long to be remembered in their history. It was characterized as a day of wondrous grace. The exercises of the hour were broken off to hear the reasons for the hope of those who wanted to join the church. The following Sabbath eleven were baptized by Bro. Ansley. It was thought this was the most powerful day that had been seen in Chester for some time. A gracious revival was in full force, some manifested their interest in the Savior every night. Nov. 28th, thirteen more were baptized, Bro. Dimock and Ansley administered the ordinance at the same time, when one went into the water the other came out. On the first Sabbath in December seven more were baptized and *several restored to church fellowship*. December the twelfth five more were baptized. "What God hath wrought!" they exclaimed, "What wonders of mercy do we see!"[21] (Emphasis added.)

FOR FURTHER REFLECTION . . .

Meditation

Remember our history, friends, and be warned. All our ancestors were led by the providential Cloud and taken miraculously through the Sea. They went through the waters, in a baptism like ours, as Moses led them from enslaving death to salvation life. They all ate and drank identical food and drink, meals provided daily by God. They drank from the Rock, God's fountain for them that stayed with them wherever they were. And the Rock was Christ. But just experiencing God's wonder and grace didn't seem to mean much—most of them were defeated by temptation during the hard times in the desert, and God was not pleased.

The same thing could happen to us. We must be on guard so that we never get caught up in wanting our own way as they did. And we must not turn our religion into a circus as they did— "First the people partied, then they threw a dance." We must not be sexually promiscuous—they paid for that, remember, with 23,000 deaths in one day! We must never try to get Christ to serve us instead of us serving him; they tried it, and God launched an epidemic of poisonous snakes. We must be careful not to stir up discontent; discontent destroyed them.

---

21. Ibid., 4.

These are all warning markers—danger!—in our history books, written down so that we don't repeat their mistakes. Our positions in the story are parallel—they at the beginning, we at the end—and we are just as capable of messing it up as they were. Don't be so naive and self-confident. You're not exempt. You could fall flat on your face as easily as anyone else. Forget about self-confidence; it's useless. Cultivate God-confidence.

No test or temptation that comes your way is beyond the course of what others have had to face. All you need to remember is that God will never let you down; he'll never let you be pushed past your limit; he'll always be there to help you come through it. (1 Cor 10:1–13, *The Message*)

Thought

All the strength that may come through prayer comes from the goodness of God, for he is the goodness of everything . . . for the highest form of prayer is to the goodness of God.[22]

Jesus demonstrates the truth of this statement in his intentional devotion to prayer, which inspired the disciples to ask for lessons on prayer (Luke 11).

Questions for Personal and Group Reflection

(1) According to the *Apostolic Constitutions*, how and why was discipline practiced in the early church? Which of the principles identified do you think could be applied today?

(2) "Salt and light" is a metaphor Jesus used to describe the effect Christian disciples should have in their culture. How were the Genevan and German Reformed churches change agents in their societies? What might be learned from them?

(3) What were the main motives identified in this chapter for Christian discipline among congregations in the Free Church tradition—Baptists, Methodists, and Presbyterians? What lessons might be gleaned from their practices?

(4) What can be learned from the practice of discipline in the nineteenth-century Chester Baptist Church and the Association to which it belonged? Discuss their motives and disciplinary methods.

---

22. Julian of Norwich, "The Highest Form of Prayer," 77.

6

Matthew 18: Blueprint for Christian Discipline

It has been said that the continuity of the church depends as much on discipline as on truth.[1] Discipline, motivated by genuine concern for the spiritual well-being of the believers, serves the larger goal of maintaining the divinely initiated and ordered covenant relationship between God and his people, and the covenant relationship of the people with one another. As one writer has put it:

> Discipline has sometimes to be exercised for the sake of the Church. To shut our eyes to offences is not always a kind thing to do; it may be damaging. A poison must be eliminated before it spreads; a weed must be plucked out before it pollutes the whole ground. Here we have a whole principle of discipline. Discipline should never be exercised for the satisfaction of the person who exercises it, but always for the mending of the person who has sinned and for the sake of the Church. Discipline must never be vengeful; it must always be curative and prophylactic.[2]

The demeanor of the congregation should thus be one of sorrow over sin: "[I]t is the duty of every Church to mourn over the faults of individual members, as domestic calamities belonging to the entire body... [necessitating] a pious and dutiful correction... inflamed with holy zeal through displeasure at the offence; in fear of otherwise severe judgment."[3]

---

1. Carson, "Matthew," 374.
2. Barclay, *The Daily Study Bible: The Letter to the Corinthians*, 45, 46.
3. Calvin, *Commentary on the Epistles of Paul to the Corinthians*, 195.

MATTHEW 18: CHRISTIAN DISCIPLINE OUTLINED

The Gospel of Matthew explicitly outlines a method for Christian discipline, asserting that it is indispensable for the ordering of right relationships within the covenant community whose members exercise mutual care. This outline, presented by Matthew (18:15–22) as Jesus' instruction as to how this ministry should be exercised, is contextualized by being placed in the midst of a series of vignettes about relationships. The disciples are told that if they would be great, they must become like children, and they are then admonished to avoid causing "these little ones who believe in me to sin," an exhortation to protect those most dependent and vulnerable in the community (Matt 18:1–10). Matthew then paints the picture of the shepherd seeking after the lost sheep, "the one that went astray," defenseless, vulnerable, needing care, protection, and rescue (Matt 18:12–14), sought after even when the other ninety-nine are safe.

Then, in verse 15, the description of how Christians are to deal with those who have sinned begins: the description of a process, not a single event. The implication of the entire pericope is that Christians in the family of God the Father are dependent on one another, just as children are dependent on adults, and sheep are dependent on shepherds. Wandering disciples need to be sought after and restored. Every effort must be made, by individuals and by the whole assembly, to bring erring family members back into the fold. The family must work to show erring family members the "limitless grace and forgiveness of the father"[4]:

> "If your brother sins against you,[5] go and tell him his fault, between you and him alone. If he listens to you, you have gained your brother. But if he does not listen, take one or two others along with you, that every word may be confirmed by the evi-

---

4. Gibbs, *Concordia Commentary*, 892–96. Gibbs argues that the occurrence of sin in the church inevitably causes or results in broken or damaged relationships within the fellowship, and that discipline therefore inevitably has both individual and corporate implications. Gibbs notes the shift from the singular "you" in vv. 15–18 to the plural form in vv. 19–20, as well as the graduated responsibility for mutual member care; the patient, persistent process outlined, with no reference to timeline, in providing radical inclusive care, with a view to retention, rescue, repentance, and restoration in faith. (It is suggested that even the reference to exclusion might be interpreted as radical love or a form of earnest, caring evangelism.)

5. Most major New Testament manuscripts exclude, or at least question the inclusion of, the words "against you" in this verse.

dence of two or three witnesses. If he refuses to listen to them, tell it to the church; and if he refuses to listen even to the church, let him be to you as a Gentile and a tax collector. Truly, I say to you, whatever you bind on earth shall be bound in heaven, and whatever you loose on earth shall be loosed in heaven. Again I say to you, if two of you agree on earth about anything they ask, it will be done for them by my Father in heaven. For where two or three are gathered in my name, there am I in the midst of them." Then Peter came up and said to him, "Lord, how often shall my brother sin against me, and I forgive him? As many as seven times?" Jesus said to him, "I do not say to you seven times, but seventy times seven." (Matt 18:15–22)

The chapter ends with the parable of the unmerciful servant (Matt 18:23–35), in which the process and method of Christian discipline laid out in the preceding verses are affirmed as consistent with the character of the kingdom of God, with the divine perspective of life under kingdom authority that is outlined in the entire chapter.[6] Matthew arguably here took the liberty of interpreting Jesus' teaching to address pastoral concerns, showing his own understanding of Jesus' heart and his pastoral approach to the human problems of disobedience and obedience, rebellion and holiness, sin and restoration.

FIRST THINGS FIRST: BUILDING STRONG BONDS OF FELLOWSHIP

Before moving to an analysis of the process of discipline laid out in Matthew 18, it is important to underscore the basis on which such discipline must rest: *formative discipline*. Education of the believers in the basic truths of the faith, in ways of righteous living, in mutual loving care and accountability, helps to build the fellowship upon a solid foundation such that it will undertake reformative discipline when necessary, which discipline is accepted willingly or, in the best case, supported wholeheartedly. It has been commented by some that ". . . our efforts have been to develop a theology of dis-fellowship before we have ever discussed a theology of fellowship … We need to put focus on having the right kind of relationship. If we do it, there will be less need to withdraw fellowship. Or if we have to withdraw it, at least there will be something

---

6. Carson, "Matthew," 395–96.

to withdraw."⁷ This is discipline predominantly as *paideia*—formative training of the faith community in godliness and life in fellowship. Such a fellowship would work to create an atmosphere of belonging, even a "culture of confession" wherein, on the basis of James 5:16, the ". . . church offers a variety of opportunities for confession: general confession during each worship service, invitations to go to a prayer minister near the end of a worship service, 'prayer cells' made of three people of the same sex, small groups for 'life-controlling issues,' and formal confession to a pastor."⁸ Surely this nurturing of the body in mutual care will encourage the creation of a climate of both compassion for those who stray and openness to correction on their part.

ADMONITION IN THE HOPE OF RETENTION

In Matthew 18, verses 15–17 outline the process of admonition, identified as the action that should be taken in response to the sin of a fellow member of the community of faith. The English word "admonish" is a common translation of the Greek word *noutheteō*, meaning to "correct," "warn," or "put in mind."⁹ Other shades of meaning include "to exhort" or "bear influence" upon the feelings, mind, and will of another, with the intention of prompting the individual to conform to accepted behavior, or to observe a certain previously abandoned code of faith and conduct.¹⁰ In the Septuagint, the word *noutheteō* is found especially in the book of Job; the active and passive forms of the verb used to describe the act of instruction—(4:3) "being taught," "learning," "considering," or "gaining insight and understanding" from others (Job 23:15; 34:16, 36:12; 37:14; 38:18).¹¹

All New Testament occurrences of *noutheteō*—or of its nominal form, *nouthesia*—in the writings of the apostle Paul reflect his pastoral concern for the well-being of the people of God, which concern is manifest in the ongoing instruction and admonition of the believers (Acts 20:31; Rom 15:14; 1 Cor 4:14; 10:11; Eph 6:4; Col 1:28, 3:16; 1 Thess 5:12,14; 2 Thess 3:15; Titus 3:10). The goals of discipline were

---

7. Price, "Church Discipline and Reconciliation," 703.
8. Miller, "Church Discipline for Repetitive Sin," 39–41.
9. Rienecker and Rogers, *Linguistic Key to the Greek New Testament*, 398.
10. Selter, "Exhort," 567.
11. Ibid., 568.

unity of fellowship and purity of life in keeping with established biblical principles. Paul's warning to the community in 1 Corinthians 10, citing Israel's experience of discipline for its apostasy, links the two Testaments by explicitly calling believers to the same standards as bound their predecessors, and by describing the precedent of God's holding his people accountable for their behavior. In the New Testament, admonishment is thus inseparably linked with teaching, a dual thrust motivating and fostering "maturity in Christ" (Col 1:28).[12] Furthermore, as the intention of discipline is to facilitate the offender's reclamation, the nature and seriousness of his or her sin is not the most significant factor in the application of discipline; it should not determine the appropriate method or degree of discipline. What is determinative is the attitude of the offender.[13]

THE ROLE OF THE PASTOR IN ADMONITION

Admonition is the spiritual task of the entire church, directed to members who require correction from sinful behavior, and who face removal from the fellowship if such correction is rejected.[14] However, while it is the responsibility and prerogative of all members, admonition (including both instruction and reproof) is more specifically a primary responsibility of the pastoral office. Acts 15:1–35, Ephesians 4, and 1 and 2 Timothy all provide instructions to church leaders concerning their responsibility for the congregation. From the pulpit, and through compassionate but firm, biblically sound teaching and preaching, the pastor is to nurture the congregation in ways that will equip its members for the invaluable ministry of mutual member-care (Eph 4:11–16), a ministry crucial to the encouragement or stimulation of holy living (Heb 10:24–25), as well as to the reproval of those whose lives are out of line with kingdom standards of behavior.

The pastor who becomes aware of sins or schisms in the congregation should take every opportunity to publicly address and emphasize the principles involved in the particular situation. In public, the pastor should avoid any reference to the specific facts of the situation and not offer a personal opinion as to the guilt or innocence of any party. By do-

---

12. Ibid., 568.
13. Jeschke, *Discipling in the Church*, 37–40.
14. Ibid., 569.

ing this, the individual(s) involved may be better able to see the pastor as impartial, and that may encourage those involved to be more open to hearing the gospel principles the pastor wishes to share, in order that the principles may influence their consciences, judgments, and actions. The pastor is thus also more likely to retain influence with all members, influence that can be wielded for the good of the church, should there be a need for some kind of formal church meeting or hearing about the matter. In addition, such a position may help to avoid the formation of a faction that would oppose the pastor, embitter his or her experience, cripple his or her influence, and end in the severance of the pastoral relationship.[15]

REMOVAL (EXCOMMUNICATION) IN THE HOPE OF RESTORATION

The goal of Christian discipline is always reconciliation and restoration; the hope is that the offending party will respond by repenting of the behavior and being restored to fellowship—"if he listens to you, you have gained your brother" (Matt 18:15). The apostle Paul describes the desired Christian attitude in approaching this ministry, encouraging the spiritually mature Christian to be humble and gentle, keeping the future and one's own personal vulnerability to sin in mind (Gal 6:1–5), and seeking to "restore [the fallen sister or brother] in a spirit of meekness" (Gal 6:1). Where such approaches are resisted or rejected, however, the church's response must include the possible suspension or removal of the person from the fellowship altogether through excommunication:[16] "The rights and privileges that are withdrawn are meant to cause sorrow and shame to the point of repentance, and such repentance is meant to lead to requests for forgiveness and restoration to the excluding body."[17]

An example of the need for urgent and serious action is seen in the situation of the church at Corinth (1 Cor 5; 2 Cor 2:5–11). Paul tells the believers that their membership and ministry are at risk if offenders are not disciplined appropriately, exhorting them to action in the quest of spiritual purity, lest the faith community fall into disarray or be destroyed:

---

15. Mell, *Corrective Church Discipline*, 60–61.
16. Selter, "Exhort," 568, 569.
17. Baker, *Beyond Forgiveness*, 65.

> Let him who has done this be removed from among you... When you are assembled, and my spirit is present, with the power of our Lord Jesus, you are to deliver this man to Satan for the destruction of the flesh, that his spirit may be saved in the day of the Lord Jesus. Your boasting is not good. Do you not know that a little leaven leavens the whole lump? Cleanse out the old leaven that you may be a new lump, just as you really are unleavened. For Christ, our paschal lamb, has been sacrificed. Let us, therefore, celebrate the festival, not with the old leaven, the leaven of malice and evil, but with the unleavened bread of sincerity and truth. (1 Cor 5:2b, 4b–8)

Paul's direction to "... deliver this man to Satan for the destruction of the flesh, that his spirit may be saved in the day of the Lord Jesus" might be interpreted to mean excommunication—isolation from the spiritual security of the faith community, which isolation should prompt repentance and a desire for restoration. Furthermore, the reference to destruction of the flesh might mean severance from the physical safety of the fellowship and surrender and exposure to the destructive assaults of Satan, which might ultimately result in death, one of the consequences of sin, of which Satan is also the author.[18]

The seriousness of the failure to discipline has been characterized this way:

> The ultimate disciplinary act of excommunication aims at both i) etching out the awesome issue involved, leading still to restoration of the severed membership; ii) maintaining the integrity of the church—for the body not only risks spreading rebellion when instances of it are ignored (1 Cor 5:7), but is blemished before the world by sins winked at (Jude 5–13). Moreover, God himself is blasphemed by the Christian's unrepented misbehavior (Rom 2:23–24). Discipline due but ignored is not love but sentimentality, love's counterfeit.[19]

Beyond Excommunication, Love Continues

It is critical to highlight what might well be lost in the application of this sanction of excommunication. Jesus' instruction to Peter about forgiving seventy times seven suggests clearly that the church has a con-

---

18. McDonald, "Introduction to I Corinthians," 245–366.
19. De Koster, "Church Discipline," 238.

tinuing responsibility toward the individual, albeit at a different level, even after excommunication. Rather than regarding it as a heartless and irrevocable severing of relationship, excommunication should instead be seen as involving a continuing effort to ". . . regard such needy fellow disciples as the most important people of all and worthy of virtually unlimited love and forgiveness."[20] The parable of the prodigal son probably best illustrates the open-ended love and care of Christian discipline: it reluctantly releases the rebellious son, but readily welcomes the repentant one home with great celebration (Luke 15:11–32). The disciplining church is the loving church, unharnessed from the strictures of time or limitations on forgiveness. As one author has remarked, "[t]he church [makes] its split with the person . . . public and unmistakable . . . in hopes that the dramatic gesture will return them to grace . . . Church discipline matters . . . for the care of souls and for the holiness of the church."[21] Discipline, radical and responsible, expressed with grace and candor, not only serves as a "spiritual rescue mission" to those at risk, it also preserves the integrity of the church and helps define its unique role in public witness to the world—a standard or boundary of distinctiveness from the surrounding culture.[22]

In his book, *Corrective Church Discipline*, Patrick H. Mell likewise contends strenuously for a biblical approach to discipline, affirming the value of the "gospel steps"[23] offered in the Matthean formula. He commends the personal approach, first because it provides the accused an opportunity to acknowledge and confess his or her error or to explain and dispel any false accusations. Second, such an approach may increase the possibility that the individual might be reclaimed peaceably. Third, the personal approach may prevent defensiveness manifested in the defiance, resentment, pride, and anger with which someone might respond if he or she feels embarrassed before others. Fourth, where there is need for supporting witnesses, they should be people who are trusted by the individual whose actions are being questioned. They may serve as arbitrators and participants in a positive resolution of the situation, or as witnesses as to the truth of the matters at issue.[24]

20. Gibbs, 895.
21. Byassee, "Dare to Discipline?," 8–9.
22. Ibid.
23. Mell, *Corrective Church Discipline*, 16.
24. Ibid., 20–22.

THE NATURE OF THE OFFENCE OR THE ATTITUDE OF THE OFFENDER?

In his book, Mell distinguishes between "private offences" and "public offences." The former he describes as issues between two individuals, and the latter as situations between the offending individual and the church as an organization. He concedes that the two might be "mixed" or confused because of unclear distinctions,[25] an admission that supports the notion that it may be more effective (not to mention more consistent with biblical teaching) to focus on the attitude and responsiveness of the sinner to the process of corrective discipline, rather than on the type or magnitude of the sin committed—i.e., "If he listens or does not listen to you" (or, as the Seven Churches are admonished in Revelation chapters 2–3: "He who has ears . . . listen to the Spirit"). In both cases, "to listen" is arguably intended to suggest repentance on the part of the offender, and the desire and willingness to resolve the issue of sin, by which he or she has broken fellowship within the community of faith, and to work toward restoration of that relationship.

MATTHEW 18 AS RADICAL INCLUSION

While excommunication obviously results in "exclusion," it is nevertheless suggested here that the Matthean pericope on discipline can and should be interpreted as an outline for and exhortation to "radical inclusion," based on Christ's instruction to Peter that he should forgive "seventy times seven." Even though excommunication is identified as not only an alternative but in some circumstances a necessity, the entire thrust of the passage is directed to the restoration of believers. Furthermore, the passage identifies discipline as indispensable to the *koinonia* of the church; therefore, a "costly forthrightness" in such matters is demanded.[26]

Indeed, theologian Stuart Murray contends that the church, as a covenanting community, is obligated to teach and practice discipline in order to regulate healthy spiritual relationships among individuals who are organically joined to form the local congregation. These members are regarded as being in ". . . covenant not organizational relationship with each other."[27] Discipline is a natural outgrowth of this spiritual con-

---

25. Ibid., 7–15.
26. Gaventa, "Costly Confrontation," 773.
27. Murray, *Through Him Who Strengthens Me*, 141.

cern for the formative and reformative nurture of the body of Christ. Murray outlines his convictions about the matter this way:

> When the body is hurt because of the walk of an erring member, it is generally overlooked by the local church members that I know. I am sure that Jesus and the Apostolic Church emphasized the necessity of church discipline. Such passages as Matthew 18:15–17 and 1 Corinthians 5:1–5 bear witness to this... it seems to me that church discipline, that is genuine biblical confrontation of sin in the believer's erring walk, is a matter from which we must not shrink. What we need to see is that church discipline is by nature restorative and not punitive. It is the greatest force for rehabilitation of unhealthy members.[28]

FOR FURTHER REFLECTION . . .

Meditation

Regarding this next item, I'm not at all pleased. I am getting the picture that when you meet together it brings out your worst side instead of your best! First, I get this report on your divisiveness, competing with and criticizing each other. I'm reluctant to believe it, but there it is. The best that can be said for it is that the testing process will bring truth into the open and confirm it.

And then I find that you bring your divisions to worship—you come together, and instead of eating the Lord's Supper, you bring in a lot of food from the outside and make pigs of yourselves. Some are left out, and go home hungry. Others have to be carried out, too drunk to walk. I can't believe it! Don't you have your own homes to eat and drink in? Why would you stoop to desecrating God's church? Why would you actually shame God's poor? I never would have believed you would stoop to this. And I'm not going to stand by and say nothing.

Let me go over with you again exactly what goes on in the Lord's Supper and why it is so centrally important. I received my instructions from the Master himself and passed them on to you. The Master, Jesus, on the night of his betrayal, took bread. Having given thanks, he broke it and said, "This is my body, broken for you. Do this to remember me." After supper, he did the same thing with the cup: "This cup is my blood, my new covenant with you. Each time you drink this cup, remember me."

---

28. Ibid., 143.

> What you must solemnly realize is that every time you eat this bread and every time you drink this cup, you reenact in your words and actions the death of the Master. You will be drawn back to this meal again and again until the Master returns. You must never let familiarity breed contempt.
>
> Anyone who eats the bread or drinks the cup of the Master irreverently is like part of the crowd that jeered and spit on him at his death. Is that the kind of "remembrance" you want to be part of? Examine your motives, test your heart, come to this meal in holy awe.
>
> If you give no thought (or worse, don't care) about the broken body of the Master when you eat and drink, you're running the risk of serious consequences. That's why so many of you even now are listless and sick, and others have gone to an early grave. If we get this straight now, we won't have to be straightened out later on. Better to be confronted by the Master now than to face a fiery confrontation later.
>
> So, my friends, when you come together to the Lord's Table, be reverent and courteous with one another. If you're so hungry that you can't wait to be served, go home and get a sandwich. But by no means risk turning this Meal into an eating and drinking binge or a family squabble. It is a spiritual meal—a love feast. (1 Cor 11:17-34, *The Message*)

Thought

Prayer is only cooperation with God's active love in besieging the life or new areas of the life of another, or of a situation . . . As in all petitionary prayer, the one who really prays must be ready to yield.[29]

Questions for Personal and Group Reflection

(1) Identify the steps recommended by Jesus for the handling of relationships broken by sin. Have you ever been involved in this kind of process or seen it at work? Discuss your response to it.

(2) What is your understanding of "admonition"? How do you think it should be practiced? How should the pastor play a primary role in its exercise?

---

29. Steere, *The Inner Springs Of Prayer*, 88.

(3) Define "excommunication." What is the most important reason for the imposition of this extreme form of discipline—the attitude of the individual or the magnitude of the sin?

(4) How does Jesus' statement in Matt 18:17, though seemingly harsh, reveal opportunities for restoration and reconciliation?

7

Christian Discipline and the Secular Law[1]

AS HAS BEEN DISCUSSED and as can be seen in many congregations, discipline is often not a valued part of the larger ministry of training believers in godliness. The individualistic mindset so prevalent in Western society opposes, almost by definition, any belief in the corporate nature of God's people and, concomitantly, in the idea that people in a voluntary association such as a church should be accountable to one another. Added to this are a fear of upsetting congregants and, especially of late, a fear of legal problems[2] that might arise from the imposition of discipline. Twenty years ago church leaders would seldom have thought it necessary to consider that they or their churches might end up in the secular courts as a result of taking disciplinary action. Today, fear of legal repercussions is one of the concerns commonly, and increasingly often, raised in discussions about the imposition of church discipline.

The most common potential intersection of churches and the secular law in relation to Christian discipline is the response of an individual (or possibly a group) to the imposition of punitive or corrective disciplinary measures. For example, in a congregation that practices Christian discipline, the failure of a member to respond to efforts at admonition and to take the steps outlined by the church toward restoration might result in the individual losing membership privileges and responsibilities or, ultimately, being excommunicated ("dis-fellowshipped"). He or she might then turn to the secular law seeking some kind of remedy.

---

1. As noted in the Introduction, while this book makes reference primarily to Canadian law, the general legal principles are relevant to churches in both Canada and the United States. The contents of this chapter are provided for general information purposes only. Churches are advised to consult with legal counsel about specific legal questions or concerns.

2. Stott, *Confess Your Sins*, 28–30.

Christian Discipline and the Secular Law 67

Excommunication is usually a last resort, a sort of "shock therapy" that, it is hoped, will result in the erring member's repentance and restoration. And as has been stressed in previous chapters, excommunication should not be the end of the disciplinary road: Church leaders are enjoined to continue their efforts to reach erring members even after excommunication. But it is possible, and perhaps more likely these days than in the past, that a church might avoid excommunicating a member, even when warranted under the principles of Christian discipline it has adopted, for fear that this decision might result in a civil legal action. Here the church and its efforts to deal with sinful rebellion may run up against the laws of the state, whose emphasis tends to be on individual rights, while "[t]he church on the other hand emphasizes the collectivity of group interests manifested through a community of believers."[3]

People do, as a matter of fact, bring legal actions against churches for, among other things, the imposition of church discipline, and churches should certainly be careful about which, and how, such measures are imposed. In reality, however, secular courts are not in a hurry to interfere in the affairs of churches—especially not doctrinal matters—and the concerns of churches about legal ramifications of the imposition of discipline are often overblown, more the result of misinformation about the actual facts of legal actions brought against churches, and a lack of knowledge about the law and its implications for the actions of churches, and about how many of the risks of legal action might—relatively easily—be minimized.

FOLLOWING THE RULES

The first and most basic statement that must be made is that, in disciplinary matters as in others, the secular law sets out certain basic rules to which churches are subject, as they are to their own rules (e.g., as set out in the Church Covenant or Constitution and Bylaws or Operational Guidelines or Church Discipline Manual, etc.). A church cannot simply make up its disciplinary procedures as it goes along, nor ignore its own rules. Far too often, it is one of these two things—i.e., making the process up *ad hoc*, or ignoring its own rules and procedures and policies—that lands churches (as it does other organizations) in court.

---

3. Carter, *A Legal Analysis of Church Discipline in Canada and Church Discipline Update*, 90.

CHRISTIAN DISCIPLINE AND THE DUTY OF FAIRNESS

Churches, like other voluntary associations, are generally free to structure their internal operations as their members choose. Generally—but not completely. Churches, like all other organizations, are required by the secular law to act with basic fairness—surely the minimum that the biblical standard demands of them as well. In Canada, complying with the basic legal duty of fairness is commonly referred to as acting in accordance with natural, or fundamental, justice. In the United States, it is usually referred to as acting in accordance with due process.

In terms of the exercise or imposition of Christian discipline, the duty to act fairly means that the disciplinary process *must* respect and incorporate the following principles:

(1) The individual must be given all pertinent information—i.e., the complaint or "charges" or the reason discipline is being considered—preferably in writing, before or as the disciplinary process begins;

(2) The individual must be given a fair and full opportunity, at a hearing, to respond to the issues, including an opportunity to respond to, or ask questions of, anyone[4] making an allegation or bringing a charge. The individual must be given reasonable notice of the hearing date, time, and place, and should also be allowed to have another person with him or her at the meeting to provide moral support;

(3) The person or people who will make the decision about imposing discipline must be either uninvolved or have no vested interest in the outcome or, at the very least, must be people who can act honestly and in good faith, and who are committed to doing so. The individual must be informed (preferably in writing) of the decision of the church and the reasons for it.

The duty of fairness means that a church may not simply summarily call someone into a meeting on the spot to respond to a charge, particularly a charge about which the individual has been given no information in advance. A church may not bring someone into a meeting without telling the individual in advance what the agenda is. The individual must

---

4. The situation is quite different if an allegation is brought by a child or youth, as will be discussed below.

be given reasonable notice of any kind of disciplinary hearing in order that he or she may consider the matter and seek advice (including legal advice) should he or she choose to do so. The duty of fairness means that an individual has the right to know what the substance of the charges or allegations or complaints are, and who has made them, and the right to ask questions of that person. Note that the situation in which a church is contemplating disciplinary action in response to the allegation of harassment or abuse made by a child or young person must be treated differently. It will be discussed later in this chapter.

Whatever process the church decides to establish must meet these standards. The further its process is from them, the more vulnerable the church becomes to members taking legal action for a breach of the duty of fairness. The more serious the potential disciplinary measures that might be imposed (e.g., excommunication, the loss of a job, some kind of financial loss involving property, etc.), the more critical it is that the church ensure that its procedures meet these tests of the duty of fairness, because the secular law is more likely to intervene in a decision of a church when the consequences of disciplinary measures are significant.

CHRISTIAN DISCIPLINE AND JUDICIAL REVIEW

If an individual disagrees with the disciplinary action of a church—e.g., if the individual's membership is revoked, or he or she is excommunicated, or he or she is fired from a job,[5] the individual may apply to the secular courts for judicial review of the church's decision. Judicial review is exactly what it sounds like—a review by the judiciary (i.e., a court) of a decision made by a decision-making body, for example, the Board of Elders or Deacons of a church.

Judicial review is not automatic; an individual must apply to the court, and the court may agree to review the decision, or it may refuse. If the court agrees to review the decision, the court will do so on one or both of two grounds:

(1) the procedural fairness of the decision—i.e., was the process by which the church reached its decision a fair process?; and/or

(2) the substantive fairness of the decision—i.e., was the actual substance of the decision fair?

---

5. Dismissal from a job raises additional legal issues that will be discussed separately, below.

As noted above, the secular courts are reluctant to interfere with internal church matters—especially matters of doctrine—so judicial review of procedural fairness is far more common than judicial review of substantive fairness.

Here's what this might look like: Terry has been disciplined by the church and excommunicated. Terry was given only a single day's notice of the hearing at which this decision was made, was not told who had made allegations, and was therefore unable to ask questions of that individual. Furthermore, Terry believes that the church's decision is based on a misinterpretation of Scripture. Terry applies for judicial review on both procedural and substantive grounds.

Given that the substantive issue in this example is essentially a matter of church doctrine (i.e., it is related to the church's interpretation of Scripture), it is less likely that a court would agree to review the decision on this ground.[6] It is far more likely that a court would approve the application to review the decision on the ground of procedural fairness, as the situation described above clearly does not meet either the first or second standard or test of the duty of fairness.

If the court does review the decision on procedural grounds and rules that the actions taken by the church violated Terry's right to due process or natural justice, the court has the authority and the power to overturn the decision of the church. Note, however, that the court will not substitute its own decision for that of the church. Rather, it effectively sends the matter back to the church for reconsideration. The church might reach the same conclusion again and make the same decision again—i.e., to excommunicate Terry—but if the process it uses to arrive at that decision meets the three tests of the duty of fairness, then it is unlikely that another application for judicial review on procedural grounds would be successful. The moral of the story is simply this: Churches are well advised (1) to ensure that the processes they establish for the exercise and imposition of church discipline easily meet the standards of the duty of fairness; and (2) to *follow* those processes. Doing this will not eliminate the possibility of legal action, but it will certainly reduce the likelihood that a church's decision will be overturned by a

---

6. Several recent Canadian cases (not judicial review cases) have resulted in precedents that could make it more likely that courts—Canadian courts at any rate—might intervene on questions of interpretation of Scripture. One of these cases will be described below.

secular court on a review of its fairness. In fact, if the church's disciplinary procedures and its members' agreement to be bound by them are clearly documented, and if the church's disciplinary process meets the standards of the duty of fairness, and if the church follows its own procedures in imposing discipline, a court will be much less likely to intervene if it appears that a disgruntled member is seeking judicial review simply as a way of avoiding the consequences of church discipline.[7]

Remember, too, that granting an application to judicially review a decision does not guarantee that the court will overturn the decision. The court might decide that the church had in fact fulfilled its obligations in terms of the duty of fairness and that it should not interfere with the church's decision. This is what one court had to say about the excommunication of a member by a church: "[W]hen a congregation is faced with a dissident member who chooses disobedience rather than obedience, who chooses not to ascribe to, or be governed by his church, whether that be in spiritual or temporal terms ... they have the right to expel that member; to expel him, provided it is done fairly and within the precepts laid down in the rules of the church, and by a majority of the members of a particular congregation."[8]

CHRISTIAN DISCIPLINE AND EMPLOYMENT LAW[9]

As noted above, if someone who does work for a church—and is paid for that work—is dismissed from his or her position as a result of a breach of church discipline, he or she could apply for judicial review of the decision. Given that the loss of a job is a significant, potentially devastating matter, the chances are good that a court would agree to hear the matter.

If, however, the individual in question is an employee of the church *for purposes of employment law*,[10] then he or she might instead decide to

---

7. Carter, *A Legal Analysis of Church Discipline in Canada and Church Discipline Update*, 93–94.

8. *Lakeside Colony of Hutterian Brethren v. Hofer*, (1989), 63 D.L.R. (4th) 473, at 487, overturned by the Supreme Court of Canada, *Lakeside Colony of Hutterian Brethren v. Hofer*, [1992] 3 S.C.R. 165.

9. Note that employment law in the United States is different from employment law in Canada. Churches are advised to seek legal advice as to the law in their jurisdiction.

10. The qualifying phrase "for purposes of employment law" was added to this sentence because it is not always as clear as people might think it is just who is and who is not an employee "under the law." For example, historically, courts in the common law tradition (the UK, Canada, the US) often ruled that clergy were *not* employees

sue the church for wrongful dismissal. In order to support its decision to fire an employee because of a breach of discipline, the church would have to show that any employee in that position was clearly and explicitly required to abide by the church's standards and that the employee had clearly and explicitly agreed to be bound by them and to abide by the church's exercise of Christian discipline. The requirement should be outlined in the church's Constitution and Bylaws (or equivalent fundamental governance documents), and the same provision should be included in letters of agreement or employment contracts. It should likewise be made explicit and identified, in writing, to prospective employees during the hiring process and included in job descriptions and in operational manuals such as the personnel policy.

CHRISTIAN DISCIPLINE AND HUMAN RIGHTS LAW

It is also possible that the imposition of church discipline, in particular in relation to issues of sexual morality, might give rise to a human rights complaint: evidently, whether or not this might happen in a particular church depends on the specific law or laws governing the jurisdiction in which the church is situated. Churches should be familiar with the requirements of human rights legislation in the jurisdiction in which they are located and should seek legal advice about these issues.

Here's an example of a situation that might give rise to a human rights complaint: Suppose a paid or unpaid[11] staff member of a church is living with someone in a common-law relationship. If the church dismissed the person from his or her position because this lifestyle breaches the Statement of Faith or Covenant, that person might bring a complaint under human rights legislation, alleging that the church is discriminating against him or her, in relation to employment, on the basis of his or

---

of the churches they served—even though they received payment for doing so—and, as a consequence, that they were not entitled to the benefits or the protections of employment law. This is changing, especially as more and more clergy are involved with the day-to-day administration and management of churches, including supervising other staff members. But it should not simply be taken for granted that an individual—especially pastors or other members of the clergy—would be considered an employee by the courts *for purposes of employment law*. Churches should seek legal advice on such matters.

11. It is well established in Canadian case law that volunteers are considered "employees" *for purposes of human rights law*, although generally they are *not* considered "employees" *for purposes of employment law*.

her "marital status," which is a prohibited ground of discrimination in many jurisdictions. Another example is related to sexual orientation. If a church brings disciplinary action against a paid or unpaid staff member because he or she is involved in a same-sex relationship and, as a result of that action, dismisses the individual from his or her position with the church, then that individual might bring a human rights complaint, alleging that he or she had been discriminated against, in relation to employment, on the basis of a prohibited ground of discrimination (sexual orientation).

In Canada, in order to justify the imposition of a disciplinary measure such as firing someone (paid or unpaid) on the basis of a characteristic which is protected under human rights law (as marital status and sexual orientation are in all jurisdictions in Canada), the church would have to be able to prove that abiding by the moral standards or lifestyle requirements the church has established is a *bona fide* occupational requirement of that particular position. In order to be a *bona fide* occupational qualification, it would have to be imposed in good faith, honestly, and in the sincere belief that it is necessary for the performance of the job and not for any ulterior reason. The qualification must also be objectively necessary to the performance of the job.[12]

Christian Discipline and Bona Fide Occupational Qualifications of Positions

The simplest situation, of course, is for the church to require that all clergy, lay leaders, all members of staff, and all members abide by its standards of discipline.[13] However, there are situations in which this may neither be necessary nor enforceable. For example, if a church employs a gardener or caretaker whose work does not include (or explicitly excludes) ongoing or prolonged contact with the members of the church, then the church may be hard-pressed to justify that being subject to the church's Christian discipline standards and measures is a *bona fide* oc-

---

12. The standards were laid down in a Supreme Court decision, *The British Columbia Government and Service Employees' Union v. The Government of the Province of British Columbia as represented by the Public Service Employee Relations Commission* (1999, S.C.J. No. 46, at para. 54), and have been reiterated in the Divisional Court (Ontario) judgment in *Ontario Human Rights Commission v. Christian Horizons*, 2010 ONSC 2105 (CanLII), also known as the *Heintz* decision.

13. Carter, *A Legal Analysis of Church Discipline in Canada and Church Discipline Update*, 99.

cupational qualification for the position of gardener or caretaker. On the other hand, requiring volunteer Sunday School teachers to comply with the church's standards and to be subject to Christian disciplinary measures would be logical and easy to defend, as Sunday School teachers are, by definition, in a long-term position of trust and influence over members of the church and/or their children. Conformity with the church's Statement of Faith and Covenant, etc. is a reasonable and *bona fide* qualification for that position.

Note here that the difference between the two situations is *not* whether the individual will receive payment or not—in the first instance, it may be difficult to justify the requirement in the case of a paid staff member; in the second example, it would be very easy to justify it in the case of an unpaid volunteer staff member. The issue is what the church is hiring or engaging an individual to do, not whether or not the position is paid or unpaid.

In one Canadian case in which a teacher was fired from a position at a Roman Catholic school because she had married a divorced man, the Supreme Court upheld the dismissal because "[t]he teaching of doctrine and the observance of standards by the teacher form part of the contract of employment of teachers [in Roman Catholic schools]."[14] While this case involved a school, not a church, the principle underlying the court's reasoning would be the same in a case that did involve a church. Also note the two issues identified in the citation from the judgment: (1) that churches (or religious schools) may require those who act on their behalf *in certain capacities* to abide by certain standards of behavior; and (2) that this requirement was explicit in the contract of employment. The individual in the case described above could not argue that she was not aware of it; she had in fact agreed to it by signing the contract.

Different Standards for Clergy and Laypeople?

One distinction should be noted here: When the secular courts do get involved in matters of ecclesial discipline, they have treated and may treat clergy differently from laypersons. In one such case, a pastor who had admitted that he had been involved in an adulterous affair with a congregant resigned from his position but identified that he intended to continue to be active in the community; indeed, he ". . . threatened to

---

14. *Caldwell et al. v. Stuart et al.*, [1984] 2 S.C.R. 603.

tear the church apart." The elders made a public statement (to the other churches of the same denomination in the area) about his adultery and his threats. The pastor sought a court order (called an "injunction") to stop them from publicly discussing the matter and brought a claim for damages for the harm done to him, arguing that the church's actions were an "... invasion of his private life." The court dismissed the application, finding that the minister "... was in a special class of professionals with special obligations and as such a private resignation was not sufficient."[15] The court wrote:

> In fact there are certain professions which can only be exercised if those who exercise them are answerable to and guaranteed by respected and respectable authorities. To be a priest, pastor, or rabbi, is not the same as to be a vendor of peanuts. The exercise of such professions carries with it the obligation to respect the standards of the religious authorities concerned, failing which one's credentials may be removed. And it is not sufficient to resign in order to avoid the withdrawal of credentials; the withdrawal of such credentials is just as public as their granting through ordination or otherwise. For example, it is common that the bar publishes notices of [disbarment] in case of members of the bar [i.e., lawyers] who have contravened the profession's code of ethics.[16]

CHRISTIAN DISCIPLINE AND OTHER TYPES OF LEGAL ACTIONS

Tort law is a branch of the law that deals with relations between individuals or between individuals and organizations. A tort[17] is a civil wrong (as opposed to a crime, which is a criminal wrong), and it is possible that someone unhappy with the decision of a church might sue a church, alleging a breach of tort law such as defamation of character or negligence.

---

15. Carter, *A Legal Analysis of Church Discipline in Canada and Church Discipline Update*, 90.

16. *Eglise Evangelique Libre de la Province du Quebec et al v. Vermet*, Quebec Court of Appeal, December 18, 1984, (unreported). Discussed by Carter in *A Legal Analysis of Church Discipline in Canada and Church Discipline Update*.

17. The word *tort* is French for "wrong" or error.

Invasion of Privacy, Confidentiality, and Defamation of Character

INVASION OF PRIVACY

As the New Testament's clear emphasis and insistence on the importance of the fellowship of believers—illustrated by its frequent use of the Greek word *allalon*, pointing to community "life together"—is more and more frequently and commonly disregarded, the idea that Christians belong to one another and are accountable to one another is continually undermined if not rejected altogether. As John Stott has pointed out, fear of criticism and legal problems are among the reasons for this trend.[18] Churches must recognize that in imposing discipline as an aspect of "life together," they are rubbing up against the prevailing mood of individualism, and that someone who is disciplined might believe that this constitutes an invasion of his or her privacy. Since the emphasis within the church is on the individual in relation to others (1 Corinthians 12), it is hoped that courts which consider actions based on allegations of invasion of privacy will earnestly seek to understand and respect the uniqueness of Christian fellowship and mutual accountability in making their decisions on such matters.

The law in relation to invasion of privacy is too complex to be considered here other than to note that there have been lawsuits brought on this basis, related to the imposition of church discipline, including the case cited above of the pastor disciplined after having been discovered to have committed adultery. In one American case, a woman who moved to an Oklahoma community became an active member of a church at her sister's urging. Some time later, the elders sought to excommunicate her for rejecting their admonition to end an adulterous relationship. She sued the church for invasion of privacy and infliction of emotional distress, because the church publicly discussed the adulterous relationship *after* she had resigned membership in the church. The court found that the church should have honored her resignation and not discussed the matter publicly, and it awarded her a considerable sum for the harm it agreed she had suffered.[19] The court held that ". . . the decision by the elders of the church to publicly advise the congregation and [neighboring] churches about the adultery of one of its members

---

18. Stott, *Confess Your Sins*, 28–30.
19. Laney, "Church Discipline Without a Lawsuit," 76.

after she had withdrawn from membership was an unjustified invasion of the former member's privacy intended to inflict emotional harm on the parishioner."[20]

CONFIDENTIALITY

Churches should proceed from the default position that they are required to maintain confidentiality of the information related to any matter of Christian discipline. Basically, only those who need to know (not *want* to know) information about such a matter should be made aware of it or be privy to it. Before releasing information to anyone, the church leaders involved should ask themselves such questions as these: (1) "Does the information need to be disseminated to assure other members of the church that the integrity of the collective ministry of the church is being maintained? (2) Can it be reasonably concluded that [this] information will not unduly embarrass or prejudice the reputation of the member in question?"[21] (3) Do church members or clergy or staff need to know about this matter in order to fulfill their legal obligations or their responsibilities to the church? What do they need to know about it in order to do so?

It is critical to remember that an individual is presumed innocent of a criminal charge until he or she is proven guilty in a court of law. Consequently, while the church must ensure that people fulfill their legal obligations (e.g., to report allegations of abuse against a child or youth to the proper civil authorities), and while church leaders must take reasonable precautions to protect those whom they owe a duty of care—e.g., to remove an individual charged with a crime against a child or youth from any church position in which he or she might have contact with children or youth, and to inform those in the church who need to know in order that they may take appropriate measures—that does not give the church the right to simply tell everyone of the charges or to otherwise freely disseminate the information. Indiscriminately making information public about an individual who is subject to church discipline might result in the church and church leaders being sued for defamation of character.

20. *Marion Guinn v. The Church of Christ of Collinsville, Oklahoma*, et al. Unreported trial decision of the Oklahoma District Court. No. CT-81-929 (OKla Dist. Court) Tulsa County, OKla, March 16, 1984. Cited by Carter in *A Legal Analysis of Church Discipline in Canada and Church Discipline Update*.

21. Carter, *A Legal Analysis of Church Discipline in Canada and Church Discipline Update*, 5.

DEFAMATION OF CHARACTER

Defamation has been defined and described this way:

> The tort of defamation protects a person's reputation against false statements... To succeed in a defamation claim, a plaintiff must prove that a defamatory statement was made about him by the defendant to a third person. The defendant then must raise a defence or be found liable... Defamatory statements may be either written or oral. Libel is written words (or pictures, drawings, films, etc.) that are defamatory; slander is spoken words that are defamatory... A defamatory statement is a false statement that "has the tendency to harm, injure, disparage, or adversely affect the reputation of the plaintiff..." Words tending "to lower a person in the estimation of his fellows by making them think less of him" are considered defamatory.[22]

It is obvious that divulging or discussing information about an individual (including discussing it in phone conversations, in e-mail or other correspondence, or on Facebook or other social media, etc.) who is the subject of corrective disciplinary proceedings might easily give rise to an allegation of defamation. "Truth is a complete defence..."[23] to an allegation of defamation; however, the onus is on the defendant (the one who is alleged to have made the defamatory statement) to prove that the statement is true.

A church or church leaders alleged to have defamed someone by making public statements (and "public" simply means to at least one person *other* than the individual himself or herself) may also be able to defend themselves on the basis of the principle of "qualified privilege." Qualified privilege can arise in a situation in which "... the person who makes the communication has an interest or duty, legal, social or moral, to make it to the person to whom it is made, and the person to whom it is so made has a corresponding interest or duty to receive it."[24] A simple example of this would be a situation where an allegation has been made that a church member harmed a child. The church would have an actual obligation to inform people who need to know (so that they might

---

22. David Blaikie and Diana Ginn, *The Legal Guide for Canadian Churches*, 265, 266, 267. Note that while the basic elements of defamation are the same, some of the tests that courts would apply in adjudicating a lawsuit for defamation in Canada differ from those that courts would apply in the United States.

23. Ibid., 271.

24. Ibid., 273.

take precautions) about the allegations. However, if the information is disseminated indiscriminately, with malice and not in good faith, the principle of qualified privilege would not protect the person or people responsible in an action for defamation.

CHRISTIAN DISCIPLINE AND NEGLIGENCE

Negligence is a failure to take reasonable care, which failure results in harm. Actions framed in negligence are by far the most common type of civil lawsuit. Here's an example: Someone is driving too fast, is unable to stop at a stop sign, goes through the intersection and hits another vehicle, injuring the driver and passengers and damaging the other vehicle. Those who are injured might sue the driver who caused the collision for negligence. If the driver is held liable by the court, the driver could be required to pay for the injuries and damage caused as a result of his or her negligence.

Churches are not immune from being sued for negligence. Suppose the church steps are not properly cleared of snow and ice in the winter and someone slips and falls and is injured. Or suppose the church holds a supper, but the food is not properly stored. It spoils and someone becomes ill after eating it. Both of these might lead to a negligence lawsuit. Cases of harassment and abuse by lay or ordained church leaders might also give rise to liability in negligence, if proper precautions (including screening, proper organization of programs, etc.) were not taken by the church, and if a court is persuaded that the church's failure to take those precautions effectively "permitted" the harm to be done.

NEGLIGENCE, CHRISTIAN DISCIPLINE, AND MATTHEW 18

As discussed above, in relation to Christian discipline, applications for judicial review, actions for wrongful dismissal, human rights complaints, and actions for invasion of privacy or defamation are perhaps the most common types of legal actions arising from the imposition of Christian discipline.

To date, there has been only one reported negligence action in Canadian law related to Christian discipline. It is a case in which an individual alleged that the elders of her church had been negligent in counseling her to abide by the guidelines for Christian discipline set out in Matthew 18. In this case, *B.(V.) v. Cairns* et al.,[25] the judge found the following to be matters of fact:

> An adult plaintiff, who was raised as a Jehovah's Witness, was sexually molested by her father when she was a child. When the plaintiff was 19 years of age she disclosed the abuse to a church elder. The church elder advised the plaintiff that Matthew 18:15–18 applied to her situation, and that she should confront her father directly with her allegations in front of the elders of her church and give her father the opportunity to repent. Despite this advice, the plaintiff was unable to confront her father. She was ultimately brought into a meeting with her father, which was set up by church elders. At this meeting, the plaintiff publicly confronted her father in keeping with Matthew 18:15–18. This meeting and the resulting confrontation were traumatic for the plaintiff. The church elders convened a second meeting. This meeting was a judicial committee meeting intended to deal with punishment of the father. The plaintiff, unaware of the intent of the second meeting was asked to attend and recount her story for an elder who had not been present at the previous meeting. Due to the appearance that no sanctions had been taken against the father at the second meeting, the plaintiff was left estranged from her mother and feeling that her church community had ostracized her.[26]

The young woman brought a lawsuit against the church and its elders, alleging that they had been negligent in counseling her to follow the discipline guidelines laid out in Matthew 18. The judge ruled that one of the elders had indeed been negligent in providing that advice, and that the church was vicariously liable[27] for the actions of that elder.

There is, sadly, no shortage of cases in Canada (or the US or other Western countries for that matter) in which churches or church organizations have been held liable in negligence and/or vicariously liable for abuse of various kinds. This ruling, however, stands as the first of its kind in Canada. In effect, the judge imposed liability for "negligent

---

25. *B.(V.) v. Cairns* et al. (2003) 65 O.R. (3d) 343.

26. White and White, "Recent Decision Casts Doubt on Use of Matthew 18: 15–18 to Address Church Disputes."

27. Vicarious liability is a form of civil liability in which, for example, an organization or corporation is held liable for the wrongful actions of someone (an employee, a volunteer, etc.) who is acting on behalf of that organization or corporation. Sexual abuse cases often result in the imposition of vicarious liability on an organization in respect of abuse committed by a member of the staff.

counseling"—i.e., ruling that the church and its elders owed the young woman a duty of care to take reasonable measures to avoid harming her, and that giving her the guidance they did amounted to a failure to take reasonable care, and that this failure resulted in her being harmed.

It is important to note that the same case would likely have been adjudicated quite differently in the United States, as ". . . American courts have held that 'civil tort claims against clerics that require the courts to review and interpret church law, policies or practices in the determination of claims are barred by the First Amendment ["Congress shall make no law respecting an establishment of religion, or prohibit the free exercise thereof . . ."] . . ."[28]

THE *CAIRNS* DECISION AND THE USE OF MATTHEW 18

The element of the *Cairns* decision which is most relevant to the matter of Christian discipline lies in the judge's findings with respect to the use of Matthew 18:15–18 as a guideline for the exercise and imposition of Christian discipline. The judge ruled explicitly that Matthew 18 ". . . does not apply to a situation such as this one." In reaching this conclusion, the judge did not canvass biblical evidence nor seek the advice of theologians: she accepted as fact the evidence of one lay member of the church that ". . . Matthew 18 applies to private disputes between people, such as disputes over financial matters, and cannot be applied to a serious sin against God's laws, such as child abuse . . . "[29] A commentary on the case by lawyers of Carters Professional Corporation, the largest Canadian law firm specializing in not-for-profit, charities, and church law, is worth quoting here at length:

> [The judge in this case] made a generalized finding of law regarding the interpretation and appropriateness of applying Matthew 18:15–18 in cases of sexual assault. As such, her ruling is applicable to all Christian denominations, regardless of how they actually interpret Matthew 18:15–18 or apply it within their particular belief system . . . Most pastors and clergy will no doubt be disturbed by this aspect of [the] ruling, as it appears to undermine any argument that advice, counsel or direction based on the Scriptures, or carried out by clergy in his or her professional capacity, is protected as an expression of religious beliefs which should be free from interpretation or interference by the state

---

28. Blaikie and Ginn, *The Legal Guide for Canadian Churches*, 243.
29. *V.B. v. Cairns* at para. 62.

> ... In fact the circumscribed definition of Matthew 18:15–18 which [the judge] fixed ultimately on does not accord with the understanding given to that passage by many denominations. In making a general finding as to its meaning, which may not be in accordance with the teachings of specific denominations, [the judge] lowered the bar significantly for negligence by clergy. As a result, the state may have indirectly violated religious freedoms of many if not most Christian denominations in this ruling, and may force, through the threat of clergy liability, a fundamental shift in the teachings of those denominations regarding and the settlement of disputes between members.[30]

One specific element of the judge's interpretation that deserves separate mention is the notion that the process outlined in Matthew 18 is intended to be applied to situations involving "lesser sins," for example those related to financial dealings between members. There are only two remote connections to "money" in the text; the reference to "tax collector" in verse 17 and to the "unforgiving debtor" in verses 23–35. One might try to argue that the Matthean text draws on Paul's instructions to Timothy related to "unbiased" dealing with "accusations against elders" (1 Tim 5:19–22), which follow a discussion about "finances" (vv. 16,18), but that seems very far-fetched. The commandment of Jesus seems to be made about any kind of sin: "If your brother does something wrong . . ." (Jerusalem Bible); ". . . trespass against thee" (KJV); ". . . sins against you" (RSV, LNT); ". . . wrongs you" (Phillips, Amplified); ". . . commits a sin" (NEB). Given that secular courts as a matter of course invite expert opinion from experts in a wide variety of fields as part of the evidence-gathering process, it is difficult to understand why the judge did not seek the advice of an expert (or more than one) in biblical interpretation.

Be that as it may, for the moment the ruling stands and congregations are strongly encouraged to understand the implications of this ruling, for Christian denominations in relation to "their specific interpretations of their respective sacred texts" which can be otherwise interpreted and applied by the secular court system. Similarly, clergy would be required to practice careful exegesis of scriptures that are regarded as foundational to pastoral care, and agreed upon by the particular denomination. Further,

> Christian denominations that rely on Matthew 18:15–18 should review their internal policies regarding when and how they apply this passage, as the decision . . . creates a very serious challenge to

---

30. White and White, "Recent Decision Casts Doubt On Use Of Matthew 18."

the appropriateness of using this passage to counsel the resolution of disputes between adherents. At the very least, if denominations are going to rely on Matthew 18:15–18, they should ensure that their interpretation has a sound basis in scripture and put policies in place to exclude its use where the resolution process could reasonably be foreseen to re-victimize the victim or cause greater harm, such as in the case of abuse.[31]

The *Cairns* decision is a lower court decision, and it might be overruled by appellate court decisions in the future.[32] Until such time, however, in Canada, at least, this decision ". . . establishes a precedent for liability being imposed against churches, clergy and pastoral counselors in situations where they provide negligent counseling or advice."[33] It therefore must be taken seriously by churches, both in terms of its implications for pastoral care and counseling efforts, as well as for the application of reformative disciplinary action based on the biblical text.

A FINAL WORD ABOUT DISCIPLINE RELATED TO ALLEGATIONS OF CHILD ABUSE

If a child or youth makes an allegation about the conduct of a member or church leader or pastor, or anyone else who acts on behalf of the church, the church must take action, as indicated above—i.e., by alerting the proper civil authorities and removing the individual from positions where he or she would have contact with the child or other children in the church's care, until such time as some disposition of the matter is reached. However, churches *should not* undertake any kind of internal investigation of an allegation of child abuse until the civil authorities (police, child protection services, etc.) have completed their investigations and made a decision about laying charges, etc. The reason for this is simple: An internal investigation by the church—e.g., interviewing the child, etc.—could be seen to taint the evidence and could make it difficult, if not impossible, for the civil authorities to go forward with a prosecution. Churches should check with the civil authorities before they proceed, so that they do not compromise or hinder their efforts.

31. White and White, "Recent Decision Casts Doubt On Use Of Matthew 18."

32. The judgment in the case itself has not been appealed, and the *Cairns* decision has already been cited as precedent in at least one decision at the appellate court level. *Hughes (Estate) v. Brady*, 2007 ABCA 277.

33. White and White, "Recent Decision Casts Doubt On Use Of Matthew 18."

FOR FURTHER REFLECTION...

Meditation

And how dare you take each other to court! When you think you have been wronged, does it make any sense to go before a court that knows nothing of God's ways instead of a family of Christians? The day is coming when the world is going to stand before a jury made up of followers of Jesus. If someday you are going to rule on the world's fate, wouldn't it be a good idea to practice on some of these smaller cases? Why, we're even going to judge angels! So why not these everyday affairs? As these disagreements and wrongs surface, why would you ever entrust them to the judgment of people you don't trust in any other way?

I say this as bluntly as I can to wake you up to the stupidity of what you're doing. Is it possible that there isn't one levelheaded person among you who can make fair decisions when disagreements and disputes come up? I don't believe it. And here you are taking each other to court before people who don't even believe in God! How can they render justice if they don't believe in the God of justice?

These court cases are an ugly blot on your community. Wouldn't it be far better to just take it, to let yourselves be wronged and forget it? All you're doing is providing fuel for more wrong, more injustice, bringing more hurt to the people of your own spiritual family.

Don't you realize that this is not the way to live? Unjust people who don't care about God will not be joining in his kingdom. Those who use and abuse each other, use and abuse sex, use and abuse the earth and everything in it, don't qualify as citizens in God's kingdom. A number of you know from experience what I'm talking about, for not so long ago you were on that list. Since then, you've been cleaned up and given a fresh start by Jesus, our Master, our Messiah, and by our God present in us, the Spirit. (1 Cor 6:1–11, *The Message*)

Thought

Prayer is listening as well as speaking, receiving as well as asking; and its deepest mood is friendship and reverence.[34]

Questions for Personal and Group Reflection

(1) Discuss the various types of legal issues that might affect your church in the practice of Christian discipline. If possible, seek the help of a lawyer to facilitate this discussion.

(2) What is the duty of fairness? What is its relationship to Christian discipline? What does it require of churches?

---

34. Buttrick, "A Simple Regimen of Private Prayer," 100.

8

Christian Discipline: Confronting the Tide of Modern Western Culture

CHRISTIAN DISCIPLINE AND WESTERN CULTURE

ALTHOUGH THE SCRIPTURES CLEARLY identify the unique nature and mission of the church (e.g., in 1 Pet 2, Eph 2), in the world-at-large religion and church are often regarded merely as two among many consumer goods that people may decide to "purchase"—or not. Within such a paradigm, the imposition of discipline is at the very least often seen as irrelevant, at most as an affront of sorts—consumer goods do not seek to regulate the lives of, let alone punish, their purchasers. This view of the church as just one more option in the marketplace all but demands that its ministry of mutual care confine itself to compassion, friendliness, and positive encouragement. Any notion that members of the community are accountable to one another is eclipsed or eliminated entirely because it is seen as judgmental and thus out of step with the times, and because of the secular world's virtual idolization of individualism and individual rights.

The church that takes the ministry of Christian discipline seriously must therefore recognize and accept that it is fighting an uphill battle against the tide of Western culture: it must make a conscious, deliberate choice to educate, train, and form the believers in kingdom living, within a community that demands, and practices, mutual accountability.

> Discipline, morality . . . are learned characteristics . . . Training is important because it involves the formation of the self through submission to authority that will provide people with virtue necessary to make judgments . . . In order to be moral, to acquire

knowledge about what is true and good, a person has to be made into a particular kind of person. Therefore, transformation is required if one is to be moral at all. In short, no account of moral life is intelligible that does not involve some account of conversion . . . especially conversion from [secular] liberal convictions.[1]

This clash of cultures can be seen clearly in the story of the differences between Moravian Brethren communities in Germany and in Salem, North Carolina in the late eighteenth century. In the German community, Matthew 18:15–20 was the basis of community discipline. Spiritual freedom was the basic goal, and it was seen to require ". . . submission to the good of the whole and obedience to Christ as literal Lord of the community."[2] Although such a disciplined community might appear to others as a rigid and joyless place, to be shunned in favor of the environment within which one can do as one pleases, it can be—and was here—understood otherwise:

> In a sense, the statutes . . . served as a specific blueprint for life in the baptized town. The Salem statutes [patterned after a European model] encompassed both the life of the Spirit and the life of the flesh. They provided a measure by which to discipline human weakness, but they were drawn up for a people in whom the Holy Spirit was assumed to be working towards sanctification and providing continual strength to resist evil. Under these circumstances, all activity was to be guaranteed by a spirit of brotherly love. The statutes held no room for renegade individualism and little room for conflict.[3]

Over time, however, as the notion of individualism took hold in American culture, members of succeeding generations began to resist the application of these principles. In addition, revivalism, with its emphasis on individual salvation, and the Enlightenment, with its emphasis on self-fulfillment, began to seriously erode the commitment to the communal aspect of fellowship. Fast-forward to the twentieth century, with its championing of the rights of the individual over those of the collectivity, as well as Western cultural emphases such as "self-confidence," "self-realization," "self-fulfillment," and "self-gratification"—themes

---

1. Hauerwas, "Discipleship as a Craft, Church as a Disciplined Community," 881–84.

2. Sommer, "A Different kind of Freedom? Order and Discipline among the Moravian Brethren in Germany and Salem, North Carolina 1771–1801," 221.

3. Ibid., 224.

popularized not only outside, but inside the church, through the sermons, writings, and teachings of various theologians.[4]

Within this environment, the doctrine of sin has, in many parts of the church, been reframed and redefined as "not having oneself together" rather than as rebellion against, or alienation from, God. Similarly, the "self-help" gospel has replaced the gospel of grace, popularizing such notions as "believing in yourself," "having faith in your own abilities," and "self-confidence leads to self-realization and successful achievement."[5] Salvation likewise has been redefined as a subjective matter, something one can accomplish oneself through one's own efforts to become a "real person" through—of course—"self-discovery," "self-acceptance," and "self-love," instead of through the objective experience of forgiveness and being regenerated into a new person by the power of God in the work of Christ.[6]

These shifts either undermine or grossly distort Christian doctrine about humanity: "The basic Christian concept of the unique importance of the self was stripped of its theological justification . . . [as a result, such] traditional spiritual concepts as the Christian self in prayer, contemplation, obedience, mysticism—in faith, atrophied in twentieth century Protestantism"[7]—and not only in this branch of the church. This focus on the self, no matter how honest or well intentioned, has since degenerated into little more than a focus on ". . . a self-gratifying narcissistic world"[8] that has little place for, denies the importance of, and is actually destructive of community. Even creativity emerging from self-actualization, the highest principle in Abraham Maslow's hierarchy of human needs, celebrated and widely accepted as a truthful representation of reality, may be understood as essentially subjective in nature—again, "self-actualization" not "community-actualization" is the pinnacle and goal.

---

4. Vitz, *Psychology as Religion*, 68, 70, 71.
5. Ibid., 100.
6. Ibid., 72.
7. Ibid., 101.
8. Ibid.

THE CHURCH AS THE SCHOOL OF CHRISTIAN DISCIPLESHIP AND DISCIPLINE

It must also be said that the Enlightenment's emphasis on individual freedom and the incipient notion of individual rights contributed to the gradual erosion of the faith community's authority over its members. Conversion, for example, began to be regarded more as acceptance of a system of religious beliefs than as the first step in a process of discipleship and training in a faith, in core values and moral principles that would transform one's life. Over the centuries since the Enlightenment, the conviction that, in addition to the family and home, the church, the community of believers, is—and should be—a school for education in morals and values has been eclipsed by acceptance of the importance of a supposedly "value-free" education system. This system is largely based on the ethic of individualism, as reflected in this student's comment: "Moral values cannot be taught and people must learn to use what works for them. In other words, 'whatever gets you through the night, it's alright.' The essence of civilization is not moral codes but individualism . . . The only way to know when your values are getting sounder is when they please you more."[9]

Such a view jettisons the examples and values of Christian discipline, indeed of any religious heritage, and it ignores the communal nature of humanity and our mutual influence. It also implicitly rejects the doctrine of the sinful nature of human beings and assumes that people are basically good. Those who hold such a position are likely to assert that, because they believe truth to be relative and not absolute, all philosophies are of equal value—a position increasingly accepted by the general public. In 1990, some 65 percent of Canadian adults who responded to a national survey endorsed the idea that everything is relative; 50 percent of respondents agreed that right or wrong is a matter of personal opinion. In 1992, fully 65 percent of the youth who responded embraced this same view.[10]

WHERE THERE IS NO VISION, THE PEOPLE PERISH

How should the church respond to this state of affairs? Surely it calls for an intentional Christian response that unequivocally endorses the Bible as the basic source of the "curriculum" on values and morals and

---

9. Kilpatrick, *Why Johnny Can't Tell Right From Wrong*, 22.
10. Bibby, *Unknown Gods*, 67.

affirms the biblical emphasis on education in the church, supported at home and in the community, as integral to spiritual and moral formation (Deut 6:1–7; Ps 119:11). In the words of the African proverb: It takes a village to raise a child.

Christian education, therefore, must seek to reclaim the terrain that has suffered from the ravages of the Rogerian and Maslownian "value-free" emphasis that has been so destructive of the principles of vision and virtue. Acting from the conviction that "character education is the responsibility of the whole culture,"[11] Christian educators are encouraged to create positive moral environments which foster such virtues as pride, loyalty, and discipline,[12] encouraging the development of citizens with personal integrity for whom ". . . knowledge of the virtues—prudence, justice, courage and temperance—provide a standard by which opinions and feelings can be measured," enabling them to better understand issues and more accurately weigh moral arguments[13] as they make decisions about their lives. Youth educated in this way would be better equipped to withstand the influence of modern psychology and media, with its emphasis on "individuation and separation," which has been devastating to moral sensibilities. In the words of one watcher of modern Western culture and its impact on the church: "[Television] defines morality, shapes the sense of reality, interprets world events, conferring or denying significance according to whim or political correctness, promotes premarital or extra-marital sex and ignores or downplays religion."[14]

Another subtle and insidious impact of this "value-free" culture is the growing tendency of the individual to avoid personal responsibility for moral decisions and to refuse to be held accountable to others for such decisions. It is ironic that, in the quest for so-called "individuation and separation," individuals persist in blaming their faults on parents or others. Secular counseling or therapeutic efforts may be valuable and helpful, but they may nevertheless fail to address such important issues as guilt, confession, forgiveness, and restoration. And, sadly, Christian leaders are not immune from this disease. One pastor, confronted about his sexual abuse of members of his congregation, defended himself by offering this explanation: "[W]hen he was a kid . . . his family had been

11. Ibid., 26.
12. Ibid., 226, 227.
13. Ibid., 243.
14. Ibid., 264.

sexually repressive and . . . he was determined as an adult to overcome that and make sure it didn't happen to other people, and help people appreciate their sexuality . . . He did a lot of sex education in the community, and was known for that . . . [He] did counsel many women about their sexual problems and [argued] that he just really wanted to help women fulfill their sexuality and experience orgasm and know themselves fully as sexual beings."[15] In effect, the pastor was painting himself as the victim of his self-described "sexually repressive" family and was suggesting that his actions were actually attempts to do something good and positive.

Moreover, while the church must seek the revitalization of education in morals and values in the secular system, its primary responsibility is to reassess its own educational efforts within the community of faith: Consistency, clarity, and particularity in teaching the principles of the faith must be the banner under which the church renews its commitment to Christian education as an indispensable factor in spiritual formation and discipleship. Likewise, Christian leaders must challenge parents to make the home a partner with the church in the war for moral reformation. Religion, discipline, and a Christian work ethic form solid pillars for homes in which moral and spiritual development are inextricably linked and which seek to inculcate commitment and a spirit of self-sacrifice for the benefit of others:

> Both plants and people grow best when a good environment has been prepared for them. For the youngest and most tender plants the best environment is a greenhouse. It gives them a head start: upon being transplanted, such plants are larger, stronger, and more resilient to disease than other plants. Children need similar protection and nurturing for healthy moral development . . . The child brought up in a good home environment would be stronger, healthier, and more resistant to various moral diseases circulating in the larger culture.[16]

The church must thus take seriously its responsibility to provide a good, solid foundation in Christian teaching to all believers, not just to new believers, so that they may be equipped to make moral decisions and ethical choices consistent with the faith in a secular, individualistic culture. Again, this form of Christian discipline, which we may call for-

---

15. Rambo, "Interview with Reverend Marie Fortune, August 8, 1990," 310.
16. Kilpatrick, *Why Johnny Can't Tell Right From Wrong*, 256.

mative, is the necessary foundation for any and all recourse to reformative discipline—the right to impose corrective discipline is secondary to the responsibility to teach!

INTERNAL IMPEDIMENTS TO CHRISTIAN DISCIPLINE

Factors that undermine the efforts of the church to establish both formative and reformative discipline may come from inside the church as well as from outside. If, for example, neighboring congregations even of the same denomination do not share views with respect to discipline, an individual under discipline in one may find a place of fellowship in another, with no questions asked about previous background or faith experience. In addition, independent churches and para-church organizations that have little or no discipline may allow those who would avoid discipline easy access to their fellowship.[17]

Then too, there are the examples set by a number of Christian denominations, whose current situation—divided, facing schism—the author would suggest, is at least in part the result of the neglect of Christian discipline, including formation based on a solid foundation of biblical doctrine. The undermining of Christian faith and values, including the condoning or acceptance of spiritual, moral, and ethical practices that are unbiblical can only lead to disastrous spiritual and ecclesial consequences for that church. As Paul wrote to the Corinthian church: ". . . Do you not know that a little leaven leavens the whole lump? Cleanse out the old leaven that you may be a new lump, as you really are unleavened. For Christ, our paschal lamb, has been sacrificed. Let us, therefore, celebrate the festival, not with the old leaven, the leaven of malice and evil, but with the unleavened bread of sincerity and truth" (1 Cor 5:6–8). Of the failure in one contemporary church to do as Paul instructs, one commentator has written the following:

> This failure of nerve (to discipline errant leaders) gradually opened a hole in the church that truckloads of aberrant clerics have since driven through. They have endorsed everything from premarital sex [during the values clarification sex-education era] to homosexual sex (beginning in the 1970s) to the worship of pagan deities (a service for which was posted briefly on the church's national website in late October 2004)—not to mention

---

17. Jeschke, *Discipling in the Church*, 148–50.

the regular and sundry denials of key church doctrines (like the resurrection and deity of Christ).[18]

In addition to the action (or inaction) of various churches and denominations, a serious impediment to the maintenance or revitalization of Christian discipline lies in the moral lapses and ethical indiscretions of well-known and highly respected Christian leaders. The manner in which some of these matters have been handled by the appropriate disciplinary bodies has not helped either, nor have the attitudes of some of the respondents to the charges brought against them. Undoubtedly, public knowledge of these incidents has proven scandalous and counterproductive to the life and witness of the church. These incidents have not only precipitated critical disruptions in local congregations, they have also dealt serious body blows to the global mission efforts of some denominations.

The reality is that church leaders must be held accountable for their conduct and must be dealt with fairly and transparently, according to the principles of Christian discipline, just as any other member would be. Otherwise, discipline is seriously compromised if not robbed of credibility altogether. Most pastoral leaders are members of the congregations under their care and should be subjected to that community's standards—they are accountable to the faith community for their behavior. Even where their official or formal membership is contested, it remains true that all believers are part of the body of Christ and are therefore accountable to the same disciplinary principles.

ONE CONGREGATION'S JOURNEY

The relatively recent experience of one congregation's journey through the disciplinary process is quite instructive. A staff member, guilty of multiple adulterous affairs, was subjected to discipline from the church over a period of just over two years, from the moment of confrontation through to eventual restoration. The process was initiated with the vision and conviction that discipline must be seen in a redemptive light: "The primary purpose" being "restoration—not retribution."[19] The disciplining body also sought to ensure that both the love and purity of God would be held in balance, as Francis Schaeffer counsels: "If we

18. _____. "Canterbury Crackup," 28–29.
19. Baker, *Beyond Forgiveness*, 16.

show either of these without the other, we exhibit, not the character, but a caricature of God . . . If we stress the love of God, without the holiness of God, it turns out only to be compromise. But if we stress the holiness of God without the love of God, we practice something that is hard and lacks beauty."[20]

Taking action in response to the sin of the pastor was a moment of truth for the pastoral staff and congregation, a veritable test of the strength or cohesiveness of fellowship and the depth of their spirituality as it related to caring for fallen believers. The first challenge was to address the situation with both firmness and genuine compassion, in an effort to discourage the offender from prematurely resigning and running from or otherwise resisting discipline, which would have led to a protracted situation without any resolution. The senior pastor recounts the discussion about this possibility: "We agreed that this sort of response would complicate the disciplinary process, but biblical action still needed to be taken in order to (1) protect ourselves from any insidious inference [his] departure might suggest; (2) protect any future church from the corrupting influence of sin; (3) protect [the church] from any form of compromise, and (4) protect [the offending pastor] from himself."[21]

The nature of the sin and the fact that it was a church leader who had committed it convinced the church that the entire congregation must be made aware of it. "Corrective church discipline is designed for sins of such a nature that they obscure the truth of God, bring into question the character of God, or obstruct the purposes of God . . . these sins are also pervasive and infectious and cause spiritual weakness to the body of Christ."[22] The congregation embarked on the corrective journey with the sincere conviction that ". . . discipline in the church is not optional but mandatory—it is an absolute necessity if we are going to be obedient to the scriptures—Matt 18:15–20, Acts 5:1–11, 1 Cor 5:1–5, 1 Thess 5:14, 2 Thess 3:6-15, 1 Tim 5:20, Titus 1:13, 3:10, Rev 2, 3."[23]

Furthermore, this biblical foundation for the process of discipline allowed the church to understand that the ministry had a number of purposes: honoring Christ, restoring sinners (Matt 18:15; 1 Cor 5:5;

20. Ibid., 17.
21. Ibid., 31.
22. Ibid., 43, 45.
23. Ibid., 33, 34.

2 Cor 2:8; Gal 6:1), maintaining purity (1 Cor 5:6–8), and discouraging others from sinning (1 Tim 5:20). It also required that members act out of love and fear for the fallen individual and for their own vulnerability (Gal 6:1; 2 Thess 3:15).[24] To be sure, the response of leaders subject to discipline will affect the overall reception or rejection of the church's restorative ministry. Humble acquiescence to the ministry of Christian discipline, accompanied by compliance, is of course the ideal.

In dealing straightforwardly with this situation, the church followed the very outline offered in Matthew 18:15–20, assuming the covenant relationship of mutual care and accountability as the foundation of effective biblical discipline, since ". . . discipline demands accountability, and effective accountability is impossible among strangers."[25] The process recognized the imperfections of human beings, making provision for failure in discipleship and the means to address it. It commanded confrontation as a necessary approach to resolving the issue, and reproof as a means of eliciting confession and repentance; it sought restoration as the ultimate goal in the process, providing immediate and extended alternative responses as dictated by the situation, and it asserted the church's prerogative for involvement in and authority over the pursuit of disciplinary efforts.[26] And, although the entire process took twenty-six difficult months to complete, with much personal and corporate pain for all individuals and the church family (Heb 12:10–11), the ultimate restoration was a joyful celebration of a moment in the journey of grace:

> When [he] fell in battle, we regarded him as a wounded soldier. We rushed to his aid and attempted to help him up. He responded beautifully. He let us help him. We loved him and we watched him as he responded to the grace of God and the love of the church family in a way that I've never seen demonstrated before. For two years and two months we watched the Spirit of God at work in him and through him and in us and through us, restoring a man to active ministry.[27]

This model of restorative ministry demonstrates that where corrective discipline demanded that the offender humble himself, his restoration required celebration. If, however, the person under discipline proudly

24. Ibid., 34, 35.
25. Ibid., 66.
26. Ibid., 35–42.
27. Ibid., 96.

refuses to comply, confusion, protracted bitterness, and, sometimes, litigation may result, culminating in the leader's departure, a possible split in the church or, more seriously, a rift in the entire denomination.

Discipline, then, is the spiritual housekeeping effort undertaken for "soul maintenance." It is both preventive and corrective in function, and it is indispensable to the spiritual health of individual believers and communities of faith. It is a lifelong process of daily living in The Presence or walking in step with the Spirit. The church that will remain healthy and growing must be courageous in its commitment to disciplinary practices, in spite of possible ridicule and misunderstanding. In so doing, the church shall remain strong and will be less vulnerable to the many evils that prevail in the world.

FOR FURTHER REFLECTION . . .

Meditation: Place Your Life Before God

> So here's what I want you to do, God helping you: Take your everyday, ordinary life—your sleeping, eating, going-to-work, and walking-around life—and place it before God as an offering. Embracing what God does for you is the best thing you can do for him. Don't become so well-adjusted to your culture that you fit into it without even thinking. Instead, fix your attention on God. You'll be changed from the inside out. Readily recognize what he wants from you, and quickly respond to it. Unlike the culture around you, always dragging you down to its level of immaturity, God brings the best out of you, develops well-formed maturity in you. (Rom 12:1–2, *The Message*)

Thought

> Even when our heart is cold and our mind is dim, prayer is still possible to us. "Our wills are ours, to make them thine" . . . The determined fixing of our will upon God, and pressing toward him steadily and without deflection; this is the very center and heart of prayer.[28]

---

28. Underhill, "What Do We Mean By Prayer?," 115.

Questions for Personal and Group Reflection

(1) Name the major external obstacles to the practice of Christian discipline that churches must confront.

(2) What are the internal obstacles to the practice of Christian discipline within churches?

(3) What is the most crucial challenge for churches in relation to the implementation of Christian discipline?

(4) What lessons can be learned from the example of the pastor who was disciplined over a period of more than two years? What reasons did church leaders give for following Matthew 18 as the process for disciplining the pastor? Discuss your personal views about the process: What might have been done differently?

9

Establishing the Ministry of Christian Discipline: The First Three Pillars

Having outlined the basic shape of the secular legal issues that seem to frighten many churches away from establishing and exercising the ministry of discipline, and having discussed the urgent need to counteract many elements of prevailing Western culture that undermine its exercise, we now turn to consider the first three pillars of a strategy which churches might employ in seeking to establish or re-establish it, as well as the primary resources and instruments that may aid in this task.

THE FIRST PILLAR: THE BIBLE

The most important "resource" of all, of course, is the Holy Bible, the basic source of knowledge of the standards of faith and conduct for those who believe in Jesus Christ. There is no doubt that the church must struggle against the culture of individualism, relativism, and commercialism, and it must also be concerned about the potential impact of the secular law upon its activities. It must be admitted, however, that there is a prevailing reality *within* many churches which undermines or impedes the practice of the ministry of Christian discipline—that is, the lack of knowledge and understanding of the basic biblical principles underlying, calling for, and describing Christian discipline as a formative and reformative means of maintaining the spiritual health of individual believers and the body of Christ.

Biblical Discipline and Spiritual Transformation

The Bible presents discipline first and foremost as an experience of transformation, and in this transformation spiritual formation begins.

Establishing the Ministry of Christian Discipline: The First Three Pillars

It is through the renewed Christian mind that disciples of Christ may cultivate ". . . the eternal perspective . . . [and] bring a totally different frame of reference to bear upon all that touches human success or human failure, human joy or human misery, human health or human pain."[1] This appeal, first heard years ago, speaks just as loudly to the contemporary situation, clamoring for the deliverance of the Christian mind from bondage to the currents of prevailing culture and seeking a return to a Christian worldview. It is a perspective which includes the unashamed affirmation of the reality of heaven and hell, time and eternity, and humanity and creation, all having their being and destiny in God, with the natural order dependent upon the supernatural order. Such a mind seeks to understand and cultivate the eternal perspective of a loving, sovereign God who sustains the universe and human life.

The task of Christians therefore is to embrace or re-embrace truth as objective reality having its source in God, made known through divine revelation, the truth eternal and unchanging. This fundamental notion contradicts the basic biases of secularism, with its emphases on individualism (the pursuit of one's own ends or ideas as the most important mode and principle of life), subjectivism (the idea that one's own feelings are the measure of truth), and even atomistic individualism (the view that the world revolves around the individual), all of which are deeply rooted in contemporary Western culture.[2] As indicated in numerous passages in the New Testament, spiritual transformation is the noble and worthy pursuit of every disciple of Jesus Christ (John 3:3–5;15:3; 2 Cor 5:17–21; see also Ps 24; 119:9–11), and nowhere is the call, possibility, and result of such transformation made clearer than in the exhortation of Paul in Romans 12:2: "Do not be conformed to this world but be transformed by the renewal of your mind, that you may prove what is the will of God, what is good and acceptable and perfect." This chapter, indeed, the whole of Romans 12–16 is pivotal to the discussion of the Christian mind and the need for its transformation so that it may, to the degree possible for humans, share in the divine perspective.

The Christian life begins with submission to the Lord and separation from the world (Rom 12:1, 2). This entails a conscious, intelligent, consecrated devotion to the service of God, seeking transformation "by the renewal of [the] mind," whereby the ". . . *nous*, [the Greek word for]

---

1. Blamires, *The Christian Mind*, 83.
2. Ibid., 130.

mind, the thinking power, reason in its moral quality and activity . . ."[3] of the believer is newly molded, reshaped, by the word and the Spirit of God, seeking to "put to death therefore what is earthly . . ."—i.e., those things which are unregenerate (Col 3:1–17). Under the reign of Jesus Christ, this lifestyle is to be rejected in voluntary submission of the will to Christ's Lordship, which brings a renewal of mind and perspective, and a concomitant change in conduct and behavior. At the same time, in its very grammar, Romans 12:1 recognizes the possibility of relapse into old ways, unless there is a continual and deliberate effort on the part of the Christian to live a life consistent with faith.[4]

Through the power of the gospel's transformative truth, God offers his people ". . . powerful, resilient hope against the despair of our world, which believes no change is possible, as well as the romanticism of our age which believes change is an easy painless option." Such change "depends on an alternate vision of self in the world" which can be shaped through stories, "narratives, metaphors, and memories of biblical faith."[5] Three of these metaphors are children of God (Exod 4:22; Hos 11:1;14:3; Isa 1:2; John 1:12; Gal 4:1–7), friends of God (John 15:15), and servants of God (Mark 10:43–44; Isa 42:1–4):

> These metaphors are invitations to transformation: a child of God who is at home, adopted, emancipated, awaiting inheritance; a friend of God who participates with God in a practice of openness, vulnerability, and candor; a servant of God who is under way in obedience and risk . . . All of them invite to a restless reception of newness about to be given and press toward a new world over which we do not preside, but in which we live at home, adopted, freed, open, vulnerable, obedient, at risk. A child is always vulnerable. A friend is always at risk. A servant is always called to accountability. The relation discerned through these metaphors permits, indeed, requires a sense of self which is either unrecognized or resisted in our culture.[6]

Knowing the word of God thus leads to knowing oneself in relation to God and oneself in relation to others within the context of the church

---

3. Rienecker and Rogers, *Linguistic Key to the Greek New Testament*, 375.

4. The verb *"paristemi"* in Rom 12:1 appears in the aorist rather than the present tense, suggesting that the need to "present" or "offer" oneself is ongoing. Harrison, "Romans," 128.

5. Brueggemann, *Interpretation and Obedience*, 161, 174–175.

6. Ibid., 163–64.

in the world. In chapters 12 and 13 of Romans, Paul outlines how, being thus transformed, the believer is subsequently enabled to fulfill God's revealed will: Chapter 12:4–13, for example, speaks of accountability in community (cf. Rom 14:1–15:13). Chapter 12:14 instructs believers in the way they are to treat their enemies; verses 15–16 exhort disciples to have empathy with others; verses 17–18 forbid repaying evil with evil and call for believers to behave peaceably; verses 19–21 instruct believers to leave vengeance to God and, above all, to repay evil with good. Chapter 13 outlines the Christian's responsibility toward civil authorities. Overall, Paul teaches here that Christian believers are called together into a life of community that is founded and should be grounded on the word of God. His teaching is in keeping with principles recorded in the Acts of the Apostles describing the disciplined life in the power of the Spirit (Acts 2:37–47; 4:29–31; 5:1–10).

This is, in essence, formative discipline directed at the transformation of both character and behavior in conformity to the will of God, through ". . . an invasion of natural human reality by a supernatural life 'from above.'"[7] God's grace, through his Word and Holy Spirit, converges with the human spirit, producing a renewed individual who experiences ". . . a renovation of character, which proceeds by changing people from the inside, through [an] ongoing personal relationship to God in Christ and to one another . . . one that changes their ideas, beliefs, feelings, and habits of choice, as well as their bodily tendencies and social relations (and) penetrates to the deepest layers of their soul,"[8] thus ". . . forming the inner world of the human self in such a way that it becomes like the inner being of Christ himself."[9]

THE SECOND PILLAR: STATEMENTS OF FAITH AND CHURCH COVENANTS

The biblical call and outline must be the basis for the establishment and practice of the ministry of Christian discipline; however, the church's understanding of this call and outline should not be left undeclared and undefined. Churches are therefore encouraged to create basic documents that articulate their fundamental beliefs and set out the commitments of

---

7. Willard, *Renovation of the Heart*, 19.
8. Ibid., 15.
9. Ibid., 25.

the members of the community to one another – i.e., documents such as Statements of Faith and Covenants. Such documents may be called by other names and, indeed, some churches may elect to have one document rather than two. Nevertheless, for the sake of clarity, two documents will be described here.

Statement of Faith or Statement of Mission and Identity

A Statement of Faith[10] is a document which outlines the beliefs of a congregation or church, including but not limited to its members' beliefs in the biblical warrant for the practice of Christian discipline. Such a document might well be the same as, or an element of, a Statement of Church Mission and Identity: its purpose is to set out, clearly and explicitly, to members and non-members alike, the essential beliefs and core values of the church. This Statement is an absolutely fundamental document in the life of a congregation, one which would require an extended process of discernment and the agreement of the members to first create and then amend it. It should therefore include declarations only about those issues that are absolutely fundamental to the life, mission, and identity of the church.

Governance and operational matters as set out in documents such as constitutions, bylaws, guidelines, and policies, etc., must be consistent with Statements of Faith and Statements of Mission and Identity, but must not be confused with them. The details of how the church is to be governed and organized, and how it is to operate, including the processes by which Christian discipline will be implemented, have no place in and should not be included in the Statement of Faith or Mission and Identity.

Church Covenants

The fundamental principle of the covenant between and among believers found, as discussed in Chapters 2 and 3, in the Older and New Testaments, underlies, calls for, and sustains community discipline. It is the obvious biblical paradigm of a shared foundation for church membership. A Church Covenant, a document created on the basis of the Statement of Faith or Mission and Identity, provides a framework for

---

10. Carter, *A Legal Analysis of Church Discipline in Canada and Church Discipline Update*, 98.

the intentional relationships being entered into by those who agree to form a community. A covenant of this kind must rest on mutual consent and commitment, including consent and commitment to the practices of formative and reformative Christian discipline.

A Church Covenant may thus become a guide for the Church in the shaping of individual and collective character and guiding individual and communal behavior, as well as a resource for the education of new believers, helping all to recognize and build the church into a community of faith and mutual accountability and care, where independence and dependence blend to produce interdependence.[11] A covenant may effectively articulate the "... commitment of present and new members to specific minimal disciplines (responsibilities) of Christian life and service, both personal and congregational (responsible membership). Such a covenant should be formulated gradually and in group discussion and should reflect the specific needs and opportunities of a local church at a given time. An artificial imposition of a "standard church covenant" upon an unprepared congregation would hardly lead to the practice of vital discipleship and discipline.[12]

Covenants have taken many shapes and forms over the centuries, as can be seen in their use among early Baptists (including by exiled Baptists at Frankfurt, Wittenberg, Stoke (Suffolk), and by the London Separatists). The Church Covenant of Baptists in Wittenberg was a document with clear legal overtones. The London Separatists, Puritans distinguished by their "... emphasis on gathered or covenanted congregations," signed or verbally affirmed a similar document as a pledge of mutual loyalty to the faith community.[13] Later Baptist and Anabaptist groups adopted covenants to inform conduct, resulting in commitment "... to a particular way of practicing one's faith" and the eventual "formation of churches."[14] These covenants emphasized church fellowship, church discipline, worship, and personal devotion, and pastoral or lay care to which all devotees were spiritually and morally committed and to which they agreed to be subject.[15] They fostered the sense of belonging

---

11. Bellah, *Habits of the Heart*, 247.

12. Zeman, "Church Discipline," 18.

13. DeWeese, *The Origin, Development and Use of Church Covenants in Baptist History*, 25, 26.

14. Ibid., 32.

15. Ibid., 61.

that is created when people discover purpose and meaning in life that affirms individuality in community, a fundamental tenet of Scripture (1 Cor 12; Rom 12).

Effective covenants strengthen fellowship, affirm the sense of community, encourage commitment to the equality of all members under God, and promote voluntary commitment to mutual responsibility for one another.[16] For many communities of faith, including most Baptists, at least, the Church Covenant is a resource that has shown great potential to reorient believers to the importance of the church as a community of faith, in which accountability to one another is of primary importance: "The Church idea reminds us that in our independence we count on others and helps [us] to see that a healthy grown-up independence is one that admits to healthy dependence on others. Absolute independence (radical individualism) is a false ideal. It delivers not the autonomy it promises, but loneliness and vulnerability instead."[17] A covenant may thus be a dynamic and vital means of calling Christians to "... rethink the meaning of membership and responsible living within community,"[18] and thus is primarily a resource for formative discipline and community-building. Its value in terms of reformative discipline lies primarily in that it sets out the principles that govern the community's life together, the standards against which behavior is to be judged.[19] Ideally, a Church Covenant will help guide church members through the spiritual and ethical adventures which are positive expressions of their faith.[20] Covenants may usefully include such elements as the duty to minister to one another's spiritual needs as part of the body of Christ; and the duty to respect and submit to the authority of the church as described in the church's Statement of Faith or Mission and Identity, and where outlined in its governance documents, e.g., constitution and bylaws.[21] Governance and operational matters should not, however, be outlined in a Church Covenant document; they belong elsewhere.

---

16. Ibid., 67–68.
17. Bellah, *Habits of the Heart*, 247.
18. Cram, "An Exploration of Church Membership Beliefs and Practices," 2, 8.
19. DeWeese, *A Community of Believers*, 74.
20. Ibid., 75.
21. Carter, *A Legal Analysis of Church Discipline in Canada and Church Discipline Update*, 100.

RECOMMENDATIONS FOR IMPLEMENTATION OF COVENANTS

A Covenant is essentially the expression of a solemn vow in which believers pledge to live in organic union with one another in the spirit of Christ, as the local expression of the priesthood of all believers. It is crucial that the congregation accept the Church Covenant as a document that is biblically based and directed to the goal of producing healthy, regenerate church membership and spiritual growth, liberating individual believers both for the exercise of their diverse gifts and for communal accountability. Furthermore, Church Covenants must ensure that the principles of discipline they include are undergirded by love, grace, and forgiveness; their goal always should be reconciliation and restoration. The principles the covenant outlines should figure prominently in worship and educational activities so that all members will become familiar with them. The covenant must not be a document that remains, unread and unused, on a shelf; it must be effectively "owned" by the entire congregation and serve to help ". . . keep church members biblically sound, morally upright, and spiritually strong."[22] The Church Covenant may itself be revitalized by being used as an integral part of the reception and education of new members and by periodic review and renewals of the pledge of members to live by it.

The Church Covenant might also profitably be made part of services of recognition where public acknowledgement is made of members for faithful long-term service. Covenants might also be used at Roll Call services, or at special services held to restore inactive members, as well as in acknowledgement of transferring members.[23] Churches might also add covenant renewal elements to monthly communion or include them in the observance of special times in the church year, such as Advent or Lent. Congregations could likewise undertake deliberate covenant renewal activities in response to the changing circumstances of its life (e.g., the launch of new ministries, church expansion, etc.), and in contradistinction to the increasingly secular society that surrounds it.

---

22. DeWeese, *A Community of Believers*, 75.
23. Murray, *Through Him Who Strengthens Me*, 139–40.

Statements of Faith, Covenants, and the Secular Law

Churches as voluntary associations of individuals are, *in general*, free to create such documents as Statements of Faith or Mission and Identity and Covenants as they wish, to restrict membership to those who endorse and accept their precepts and tenets, and to then exercise or practice such ministries as are explicitly included in them, with the understanding that those who endorse the Statement(s) and/or Covenant will therefore abide by and submit to them.

To make this explicit, it may be helpful to ask people to sign a document indicating that they endorse the Statement of Faith and/or Covenant and agree to be subject to discipline as outlined in it/them. It is, however, essential that any and every individual who endorses or pledges to abide by them is giving his or her informed consent in so doing. The constitutive elements of informed consent are essentially that the individual has been given all information material to the decision, that he or she has had an opportunity to reflect and seek the counsel of others if desired before signing, and that no element of duress or undue influence has been brought to bear on him or her about signing. It is crucial that the church provide information and educational opportunities that are open and allow for thorough discussion, and during which individuals may ask questions and raise concerns, before they are asked to sign onto congregational Statements of Faith or Covenants. These are important ways in which churches can seek to ensure that the consent of individuals is indeed informed, so that they may more safely navigate what many see as dangerous seas in "dangerous times."[24]

THE THIRD PILLAR: CHURCH GOVERNANCE DOCUMENTS

With the Bible as ultimate source and guide, a church's Statement of Faith and/or Covenant lays out its basic beliefs and the principles underlying and animating the community of mutual care the church is intended to be, including its commitment to the exercise of Christian discipline. With these as foundations, the church should then lay out its governance and organizational structure such that it is consistent with and operationalizes these principles. In incorporated churches, this is usually articulated in the Church Constitution and Bylaws,[25] which

---

24. Sande, "Keeping the Lawyers at Bay," 34–35.
25. Laney, "Church Discipline Without a Lawsuit," 76.

should be consistent with the Statement of Faith and the Covenant. The Constitution and Bylaws outline the governance and organizational structure of the church, on which are based the church's administrative and operational policies, procedures, and practices, including those related to the ministry of Christian discipline. Whereas the Statement of Faith and Church Covenant are internal church documents that may be structured however the church wishes to do so, the Constitution and Bylaws is both an internal and an "external" document for an incorporated church, as it is the legal document which sets out the nature, function, and limits of the church corporation. While congregations or churches that are not incorporated as legal entities may not be legally required to have a formal constitution or bylaws, they are nevertheless well advised to establish similar clear governance and organizational structures and guidelines and to make these explicit in a document that performs the same function, even if it is known by some other name.

Separating Operational Guidelines from Governance and Foundation Documents

The governance document(s) of a church—whether a Constitution and Bylaws or some other document—should not be confused with nor include administrative or operational guidelines such as policies, procedures, and practices. Although policies, procedures, and practices must, of course, be consistent with the governance and organizational structures of the church—and therefore with the Statement of Faith or Mission and Identity, and the Church Covenant—they should not be included in those documents.

The reasons for this separation are quite simple: The Statement of Faith or Mission and Identity, the Church Covenant, and the Constitution and Bylaws (or other governance document) set out matters which are generally intended to remain fixed over the long term, not subject to continual revision (though of course they should be reviewed from time to time and amended if and as necessary). Tying the day-to-day operational and administrative affairs of the church into the Statement of Faith, Church Covenant, or Constitution and Bylaws can significantly impede the work of pastors, church leaders, and church bodies such as boards of deacons or elders, etc., who must retain the ability to make decisions, and revise plans and operational matters without every decision requiring prolonged discussion and debate or the approval of all members of the church. It is wholly appropriate that making decisions about fundamental issues such as beliefs or basic governance matters would require the involvement of all members of the church; it is not appropriate or helpful in terms of the day-to-day administration and operation of the church. The next chapter will consider operational matters as they relate to supporting churches' efforts to establish and practice the ministry of Christian discipline as called for in their Statement of Faith and Covenant, and in line with any relevant elements of their Constitution and Bylaws.

POTENTIAL ELEMENTS OF A CHURCH CONSTITUTION AND BYLAWS RELEVANT TO CHRISTIAN DISCIPLINE

As this book is specifically focused on the issue of Christian discipline, this section will include only suggestions related to that issue and not to all matters that should be addressed in a church's Constitution and Bylaws:

(1) A statement of the church's mission and identity in light of enabling or governing legislation (i.e., its legal "objects" under statutes governing religious, not-for-profit, or charitable organizations).

(2) A statement that the church in its corporate action will abide first and foremost by its Statement of Faith (or Mission and Identity) and Covenant. There is no need to restate the principles included in the Statements and Covenant here, but explicit reference should be made to them as the authoritative basis for church activities, which would of course include the implementation of Christian discipline.

(3) A statement regarding the church's intention to comply with all relevant secular law, including enabling legislation (i.e., the statute under which the church is incorporated), if any, as well as both public (e.g., taxation and criminal law) and private law (e.g., law of contracts, equity and trusts, property law, tort law, etc.). One caveat must be stated here, however. In light of the discussion in Chapter 7 about issues in the secular law and their potential impact on the imposition of Christian discipline, churches may or may not want to include this kind of explicit statement in their constitutional documents, as they may find themselves in conflict with the secular law if it contravenes their understanding of biblical teachings and

Establishing the Ministry of Christian Discipline: The First Three Pillars 109

standards or principles that are incorporated into their Statements of Faith and/or Covenants.

(4) A statement about and description of the various kinds and levels of church affiliation and membership.

(5) A statement describing the membership structure of the church, including

    (a) descriptions of categories of membership (Full? Associate? Other?), and

    (b) descriptions of the prerogatives, privileges, and obligations of the members of different categories of members regarding participation in church activities and decision-making, in particular.

Such statements should explicitly set out the situation of

    (a) Pastors and clergy: Are all pastors automatically made members of the church upon being called and hired by the church? If not, must they become full members?

    (b) Staff, paid and unpaid, (including lay leaders, volunteers for programs, etc.): Must they all be members of the church? Full members? Associate members?

(6) A statement in respect of church discipline, indicating

    (a) who is required to endorse, accept, and be subject to it. This does not mean that people's names should be included here. It means identifying the categories or groups—e.g., any and all members of the clergy, all lay leaders, all members of the church, all paid or unpaid staff and employees, etc. are subject to church discipline, in accordance with the Church Statement of Faith and/or Covenant and the privileges and obligations of church membership or of service to the church, and

    (b) that the church will abide by the principles of natural justice and due process, and will establish its disciplinary procedures in keeping with the common law duty of fairness.

(7) A statement about morality and lifestyle requirements: If the church expects its pastors, lay leaders, employees, and/or volunteers to comply with specific lifestyle or moral conduct requirements, these may be identified in the Constitution. A better option might be to indicate in it that all pastors, lay leaders, employees, and/or volunteers are required to abide by any lifestyle and morality requirements set out in the Statement of Faith and/or Covenant, as current and as may be amended from time to time.[26]

A final word of advice: Churches creating Statements of Faith or Mission and Identity, Covenants, or Constitutions and Bylaws or equivalent documents are encouraged to seek legal advice while they are being developed, so that church leaders may become aware of, and seek to avoid, potential legal difficulties their contents might raise.

FOR FURTHER REFLECTION . . .

Meditation

I, Simon Peter, am a servant and apostle of Jesus Christ. I write this to you whose experience with God is as life-changing as ours, all due to our God's straight dealing and the intervention of our God and Savior, Jesus Christ. Grace and peace to you many times over as you deepen in your experience with God and Jesus, our Master.

Don't Put It Off

Everything that goes into a life of pleasing God has been miraculously given to us by getting to know, personally and intimately, the One who invited us to God. The best invitation we ever received! We were also given absolutely terrific promises to pass on to you—your tickets to participation in the life of God after you turned your back on a world corrupted by lust.

So don't lose a minute in building on what you've been given, complementing your basic faith with good character, spiritual understanding, alert discipline, passionate patience, reverent wonder, warm friendliness, and generous love, each dimension fitting into and developing the others. With these qualities active and growing in your lives, no grass will grow under your feet, no day will pass without its reward as you mature in your

---

26. As discussed in Chapter 7, such requirements should also be made explicit in employment contracts, etc.

experience of our Master Jesus. Without these qualities you can't see what's right before you, oblivious that your old sinful life has been wiped off the books.

So, friends, confirm God's invitation to you, his choice of you. Don't put it off; do it now. Do this, and you'll have your life on a firm footing, the streets paved and the way wide open into the eternal kingdom of our Master and Savior, Jesus Christ. (2 Pet 1:1–11, *The Message*)

Thought

Prayer is more than a word spoken; it is an event to be experienced. The spirit of what happens is as important as the words spoken.[27]

Questions for Personal and Group Reflection

(1) The Bible, a Statement of Faith or Mission and Identity, and/or Church Covenant, and Constitution and Bylaws are acknowledged as three pillars that are fundamental to, and can help minimize the risk of the practice of Christian discipline. Describe the nature and value of each and its role in the ministry of Christian discipline.

---

27. Carter, *The Prayer Tradition of Black People*, 30, 31.

10

Establishing the Ministry of Christian Discipline: The Fourth Pillar

FORMATIVE DISCIPLINE, SPIRITUAL MATURITY, AND THE CONGREGATION

FORMATIVE DISCIPLINE MAY ALSO be described as the work of developing spiritual maturity, helping each individual ". . . [live] up to the capacities God made possible for [each person] . . ."[1] Those who strive, deliberately and tirelessly, to reach this worthy goal may attain it, while those not on this journey dwell in a land of "complacency and self-satisfaction" characterized by and cloaked with immaturity.[2] And while each believer must undertake this work individually, it is nevertheless also the business and the concern of the congregation, whose efforts at formative and reformative discipline should facilitate, encourage, and support these individual endeavors. Indeed, this quest is designed to be communally pursued, since Christian spirituality fails in purpose and effect when the individual is totally separate from community.[3]

As has been discussed, both Scripture and writings on Christian spiritual formation emphasize the communal nature of the Christian life. This emphasis should be embraced and encouraged as a healthy response to the dominant culture of individualism as well as to the paradoxical, post-modern quest for community: it may indeed serve as an evangelistic bridge to each. Of course, the readiness of local congregations to reach out must be gauged by their capacity to nurture such an

---

1. Hestenes, "Can Spiritual Maturity Be Taught?," 12–20.
2. Ibid.
3. Smith, *Howard Thurman: Essential Writings*, 88, 89.

atmosphere within their own ranks and their ability to provide direction to the faith community. Church leaders must model it in their teaching and lifestyle, as well as in passionate preaching and inspiring worship.

The congregation that is truly engaged in the effort to develop individual and communal spiritual maturity will be characterized by a number of features, including a genuine concern for the lost, and an equally genuine concern for the poor; by speaking the truth in love; by discernment—i.e., the ability to identify truth from falsehood, for example when religious language serves as a mask for evil intentions; by prayer as an integral part of ministry; and by leadership that sees the pastor's primary role as spiritual director (pastor-teacher, as in Eph 4:11) responsible for nurturing the congregation in spiritual growth. Such pastoral leadership offers spiritual nourishment in the context of mutual care and accountability through worship, pastoral care activities, Bible teaching, reading, and study. Other activities include the creation of small groups in and through which people may learn to pray, love, and serve one another; encouraging believers to develop Christian friendships and participate in fellowship opportunities; holding regular spiritual retreats; journaling to aid reflection on faith; intercessory prayer; setting realistic goals for spiritual growth; fostering respect for differences and diversity—including people on different spiritual journeys with different needs, circumstances, and temperaments; discerning gifted leaders and delegating responsibility to those so gifted to act as spiritual directors (Exod 18); and creating covenant groups specifically for pastors, in which they may practice mutual accountability—sharing with, and caring and praying for one another.[4]

Christian Discipline and Spiritual Transformation

Classical discussion on change and spiritual transformation in the fourteenth century spoke of two basic, inherent principles in transformation: first and foremost it is a process initiated by grace and then guided by grace. Second, transformation is also essentially communal or relational; it cannot be accomplished in isolation.[5]

---

4. Hestenes, "Can Spiritual Maturity Be Taught?," 12–20.
5. Shults and Sandage, *Transforming Spirituality*, 13–36.

Transformation might be considered to take place on three levels: functional, systemic, and redemptive.[6] The first, functional or personal transformation, refers to personal struggles such as overcoming addictions by making behavioral changes. The second, systemic transformation, involves the transformation of relationships, and may require help from others such as therapists, spiritual directors, or other counselors. The third, redemptive transformation, results from the human desire for God that is satisfied through an encounter with the Holy Spirit. The goal of this "third-level" transformation is a disciplined life conforming to the teachings of the gospel. With it comes the grace-given ability to maintain a balanced life in the secular and the spiritual realms of community and church, respectively. Both individual behavior and the communal system are affected by such transformation—e.g., people witness to their faith and transformation, the community becomes "salt and light." This ultimate transformation fulfils the goal of the Christ-event and the very mission of the church.[7]

Transformation is a continuous journey of spiritual development, which includes ups and downs, progress and plateaus, regression and repentance, and recovery and restoration. Spiritual direction is thus critical, and pastors and other leaders must be equipped to understand and implement needed intervention.[8] In effect, as spiritual directors, pastors and Christian leaders should be always seeking new ways of understanding and facilitating spiritual transformation as the primary goal of ministry, "until Christ be formed" in the people.

Christian pedagogical theory holds that most people remain at the so-called "synthetic-conventional" stage of life, in which they have embraced an unexamined faith which they are unable to explain. Life is lived to please the expectations and judgments of significant others, often resulting in a compartmentalized lifestyle wherein behavior contradicts belief.[9] In order to stimulate spiritual growth and practical faith in people, churches might consider establishing small groups to study three perspectives on faith: (1) faith as belief or conviction; (2) faith as trusting; and (3) faith as doing,[10] and in so doing seek to build an atmo-

6. Ibid.
7. Ibid., 22.
8. Ibid, 33–36.
9. Fowler, *Stages of Faith*, 151.
10. Groome, *Christian Religious Education*, 56–65.

sphere of love and understanding, and to inculcate a permanent, mutual commitment to caring and accountability, the genuine foundation for both formative and reformative discipline.[11]

REFORMATIVE CHRISTIAN DISCIPLINE

To reiterate the most fundamental principle of Christian discipline, the effort is always to be undertaken in love and in good faith, seeking reconciliation and the restoration of fellowship. Two outlines of reformative disciplinary processes are offered in this section. The first identifies the formal steps of a process leading to a decision that an individual should be disciplined. The second outlines a potential series of specific disciplinary measures a church might take in relation to an individual under discipline. They are offered here as fodder for discussion and possible starting points for the development (or redevelopment) of a church's disciplinary processes and measures. As with any other matter that intersects with the secular law, seeking legal advice about the processes and procedures a church wishes to establish is a reasonable and responsible act of risk management. Several additional caveats: (1) It is wholly inappropriate for any church to simply adopt a disciplinary process created by any individual or group or in use in another church without making serious, considered efforts to adapting those steps and ensuring that the steps are appropriate to the church's own polity, governance, and organization, and that they are utterly consistent with its Statement of Faith and/or Mission and Identity, and/or Covenant. (2) It is critical that the church is able to do what it says it will do: as was pointed out in Chapter 7, a church must abide (and must be able to abide) by its own rules, including such as govern church disciplinary matters. (3) Disciplinary action can only legitimately be imposed on those who have (a) knowingly and (b) voluntarily agreed to be subject to it. Consequently, as discussed in Chapter 9, requiring members, clergy, staff, etc. to make their agreement explicit (i.e., by signing a member's statement or agreement or by signing the Statement of Faith and/or Covenant, in which the standards are outlined) is a good risk management practice.

---

11. Vitz, *Psychology as Religion*, 91.

A Formal Process for Church Discipline

Following is an outline for a formal reformative discipline process within a church. It was created by lawyers, and it pays careful attention to the issue of procedural fairness discussed in Chapter 7.

The Sixteen Steps Of Church Discipline:

1. No allegation giving rise to disciplinary action against a member . . . shall be considered by the church unless such allegation is first set out in a signed written statement given to the board of elders indicating the nature of the allegation and providing an explanation of the basis upon which the allegation is made.

2. If the board of elders determines on a preliminary basis that the written allegation is without merit, then the allegation shall be deemed to be invalid and no further disciplinary action against the member shall be proceeded with.

3. If the board of elders determines on a preliminary basis that the written allegation warrants further investigation, the allegation shall be referred in writing to the board of elders and board of deacons (referred to as the "church board") for a hearing and the member against whom the allegation is made (referred to as the "subject member") shall be deemed to be under the discipline of the church.

4. To ensure that the remedial ministry of church discipline to the subject member and to the congregation is completed, any request or notice of withdrawal from membership in the church by the subject member while under discipline shall not become effective until after the discipline proceedings provided for herein have been finalized.

5. The church board shall as soon as possible convene a hearing to further consider the allegation. The subject member shall be given fourteen (14) days written notice (which period of time shall include the date of mailing but shall exclude the date of the hearing) by registered and regular mail at his or her last known address, of the date, time and place at which the hearing will be held as well as his or her right to attend such hearing and be heard. The notice shall briefly explain the nature of the allegation and advise the subject member that the allegation will be considered by the church board at that hearing.

6. The subject member shall be entitled to attend the hearing to listen to the details of the allegation made and to respond thereto. The hearing shall be conducted as an inquiry by the church board and the chairperson of the board of deacons shall act as the chairperson of the church board. The hearing shall not be open to the public nor to members or adherents of the church. However, the subject member shall be entitled to be accompanied at the hearing by two members of the church who may act as observers during the hearing but who shall not participate.

7. Both the subject member and the church board may call any witnesses or evidence that is relevant to the allegation being made. No party to the hearing shall be represented by legal counsel.

8. There shall be an equal allocation of time for presentations by both the church board and the subject member. The church board may designate a time limitation on the hearing, provided that such limitation is applied equally to the presentation by both the church board and the subject member and provided further that notice of such limitation of time is given to the subject member in the written notice by which the subject member was given notice of the hearing.

9. All evidence presented before the hearing shall be kept confidential, except such summary facts that the church board determines needs to be given to the membership of the church at a subsequent meeting of members.

10. At the end of the hearing, the church board shall convene in private to deliberate on the evidence presented. A two-thirds majority vote by the members of the church board present at the hearing shall be required to conclude that the allegation is true, failing which the allegation will be deemed not proven with the result that the subject member shall no longer be subject to disciplinary proceedings by the church and shall be reinstated as a member of the church in good standing.

11. In the event that the church board determines that the allegation is true, then the church board shall determine the appropriate disciplinary action to be implemented with the intent of both protecting the integrity of the ministry of the church and restoring the subject member into fellowship pursuant to the principles set out in Luke 17:3 and Galatians 6:1.

12. The church board may implement any disciplinary action in relation to the subject member that it deems appropriate, including but not limited to the removal of the subject member from positions of leadership or teaching within the church, the prohibition of offending conduct or [behavior], the requirement that an apology be given, the requirement that the subject member evidence an attitude of submission to the authority of the church or a spirit of contrition, or the termination of membership. Termination of membership in the church, however, will be deemed appropriate only where, in the opinion of the church board, no other reasonable alternative disciplinary action is available.

13. The chairperson of the church board shall send written notification to the subject member of the decision made by the church board by registered and regular mail addressed to the subject member at his or her last known address within ten (10) days of a decision having been made together with a succinct summary of the reasons therefore.

14. The decision by the members of the church board on all matters of discipline shall be final and binding. In the event that the decision of the church board is to terminate the subject member's membership in the church, then the subject member shall automatically cease to be a member of the church upon the date that the decision by the church board is made.[12]

15. No pronouncement on matters of discipline by the church shall be made unless given orally from a prepared text at a members meeting and only after careful and sober consideration has been made by the church board to avoid, as much as possible, undue or unnecessary embarrassment to the subject member or other prejudicial consequences to either the subject member or to the church as a whole.

16. A member of the church who has been disciplined or whose membership has been terminated shall not be barred from public worship services unless his or her presence is disruptive to the peaceful proceedings of the public worship service as determined in the sole opinion of the church board; in which event such individual

---

12. Note that this statement in no way nullifies an individual's right to seek redress in the secular courts.

agrees that he or she may be removed from such public worship service without the necessity of legal action, whether or not such individual is at that time a member of the church.[13]

The "Pastor Plan": Disciplinary Measures Leading to Reconciliation and Restoration

This "plan" is a model that seeks to offer effective counsel for an individual under discipline. It begins at the point of penitence and an expressed desire for spiritual reformation, and it suggests the following steps be taken:

(1) The individual is required to meet periodically with the pastor or another elder of the same gender as the individual under discipline, over a number of weeks. The meetings are intended to be open, honest discussions of the individual's spiritual progress.

(2) The individual becomes involved in a regular, weekly prayer ministry.

(3) The individual seeks counseling and consents to the counselor speaking to the pastor about his or her spiritual progress.

(4) The individual commits to asking forgiveness of the one hurt by his or her sin; a date is set for the individual to report that this has been done; the pastor checks with injured party to confirm that it was done.

(5) Depending on the sin or issue, the individual agrees to and makes a public confession to the members of the congregation and asks their forgiveness.

(6) The individual agrees to fast for a specified period of time from habits relating to his or her particular sin or problem, e.g., Internet gambling.

(7) The individual joins a small group or discipleship program with emphasis on spiritual disciplines, healing, and life transformation.

(8) The individual steps down, at least temporarily, from involvement in church ministries.

---

13. White, *Fair Play in Action: Towards Effective Discipline within the Church.*

(9) The individual agrees to refrain from receiving Communion at the Lord's Table for a specified period of time.

(10) When the pastor or elders/deacons or appropriate body are of the opinion that the individual has repented and is once again living according to the standards established by the church, action is taken, publicly or privately, to restore the individual to fellowship.[14]

Issues Related to the Imposition of Christian Discipline

Personal Information of an Individual Under Discipline

This issue has been discussed before, but it bears repeating because it is a potential minefield. The basic principle is that the church should treat as confidential any information related to an individual about whom disciplinary action is being considered or who is under discipline. That rule is not absolute, as was seen in Chapter 7 and above in the outline of formal disciplinary proceedings, but before divulging information church leaders must ask, and answer, the right questions:

(1) Who needs to know this information? Why do they need to know? Because it is required in order for them to do their jobs? Because they have some kind of legal obligation to act on this information? Because it affects all the members? Because the church is coming under public scrutiny as a result of this issue?

(2) In what forum, in what manner can this information be made available to the people who need to know it while not making it public to others? Publishing information about an individual in a church bulletin is a dangerous way of communicating sensitive information. Communicating it by e-mail is no more secure. Once information is posted online, control over it and its further distribution is lost. Is a closed-door meeting of the people who need to know more appropriate?

(3) How much information needs to be communicated? The wisest course would be to give the people who need the information

---

14. Miller, "Church Discipline for Repetitive Sin," 41. Asked why people subject themselves to the process when they could go elsewhere, the author stated, "What people want, in their heart of hearts, is to be loved so much that someone will say, 'You need change, God will help you, and I'll walk with you.'"

enough to allow them to fulfill their obligations. If, for example, a church elder is having an affair with someone, is it necessary to identify the other party? Why? If there are minors involved in the matter, should their names be mentioned? Why? There may in fact be situations when divulging such information is necessary; however, it should never be done automatically or without serious consideration of whether and why it should be done and how it is best done.

Permitting a Member Under Discipline to Participate in Church Activities

Should a member under discipline be permitted to participate in worship or other church activities? There is no hard-and-fast rule here; all depends on the circumstances and on the matter which lies at the heart of the discipline. Remembering that the intention of discipline is to seek and encourage reconciliation and restoration, it may well be that churches should permit members under discipline to worship, provided their participation is not disruptive.[15] At the same time, if the secular authorities are involved in the matter for any reason, then the church must seriously consider its obligations to comply with court-ordered restrictions (e.g., restraining orders in a marital dispute, child protection matters, etc.)

THE IMPORTANCE OF SPIRITUAL PRACTICES IN SUPPORT OF CHRISTIAN DISCIPLINE

An intentional action plan for spiritual formation of the members of a community of faith must include commitment to encouraging them in the cultivation of certain "holy habits," intentional practices of daily behavior that result in lives shaped in the image of God and Christ-likeness. Of course, such habits and practices are often themselves known as spiritual disciplines. Christian writing of the past 2,000 years is replete with descriptions of, exhortations to, and instructions for such practices. Richard Foster's *Celebration of Discipline*, cited in the Preface, is a modern classic of this genre. In this book, Foster outlines and illustrates the practice of twelve important spiritual disciplines: meditation, prayer, fasting, study, simplicity, solitude, submission, service, confession, worship, guidance, and celebration. These practices recognize the serious

---

15. Ibid., 98.

effects of sin on the human personality, manifest in the inward person and outwardly expressed in particular behaviors. This sinful nature, with its ingrained habits, becomes the target area for transformation, which is effected as individuals yield to God in submission through faith in Jesus Christ and through their intentional practice of the disciplines, no one of which is more important than the others. Indeed, Foster warns that "[t]he tendency is to isolate and elevate one Discipline to the exclusion or neglect of others. The Disciplines are like the fruit of the Spirit—they comprise a single reality . . . The Disciplines of the spiritual life are an organic unity, a single path."[16]

These spiritual disciplines are to be undertaken, not for their own sakes, but in the quest for personal, spiritual transformation—i.e., so that we may become something other than what we have been or now are. The journey of spiritual formation through practice of the disciplines acknowledges our essential nature as spiritual beings in need of specific and intentional care in order to live a fulfilled, Spirit-filled, Christ-like life. Jesus himself prayed for this, while affirming that it is only the Spirit of God which can accomplish it in the life of the obedient saint. The potential effect of the intentional, committed practice of the disciplines is wholeness (unity and harmony) and movement in holiness (Gal 5; Eph 4; John 15).

These practices are also regarded as theological disciplines, because they are rooted in Scripture and are equally part of the basic theological task of faith seeking understanding (See Prov 2:1–11; Matt 4:4; Deut 8:3; Ps 119:11,104; 19:7–11; John 1:1,14; 6:63–69; 17:6,8,14,17,20; Phil 3; Jas 1:18, 21–22), and understanding leads to being, becoming, and doing. Practice of the spiritual disciplines is an intentional intellectual and spiritual engagement, undertaken with the goal of gaining greater understanding and awareness of the nature and works of God and seeking to engender greater faithfulness and the life of wisdom. The practice of the disciplines is thus properly undertaken for the goal of increased understanding and enhanced, improved, and transformed behavior. The spiritual disciplines assist the believer to live intentionally and equip him or her to better resist pressures from circumstances and culture (Dan 1–4; Rom 12:1,2). They also serve as anchor points that prevent drifting—with every new current of thought about doctrine—from the rule of life and core biblical values that should be informing the choices made in daily life.[17]

16. Foster, *Study Guide for Celebration of Discipline*, 10, 11.
17. Zander and Willard, "The Apprentices," 20–25.

FOR FURTHER REFLECTION . . .

Meditation: Planning for Harvest

"I am the Real Vine and my Father is the Farmer. He cuts off every branch of me that doesn't bear grapes. And every branch that is grape-bearing he prunes back so it will bear even more. You are already pruned back by the message I have spoken.

Live in me. Make your home in me just as I do in you. In the same way that a branch can't bear grapes by itself but only by being joined to the vine, you can't bear fruit unless you are joined with me.

I am the Vine, you are the branches. When you're joined with me and I with you, the relation intimate and organic, the harvest is sure to be abundant." (John 15:1–5, *The Message*)

Thought

The biblical practice of Christian discipline is akin to the efforts of the farmer who intentionally, patiently cultivates the crop for maximum benefits. It is designed to nurture healthy, growing, and productive churches.

Questions for Personal and Group Reflection

(1) Discuss the possibilities for various social ministries based on Shults and Sandage's idea of levels of transformation in relation to the Bible and Christian experience.

(2) Describe the benefits of spiritual transformation in the local congregation.

(3) Discuss the elements of the steps of the "Pastor Plan" that could lead to healing and restoration.

(4) Which of the other spiritual disciplines do you think could help support the practice of Christian discipline?

Afterword

THE ORIGINAL QUESTION POSED in my thesis was whether the practice of Christian discipline was a covenant responsibility or a form of legalism. My expectation, given the issue, my experience in ministry, and preliminary discussions with colleagues, was that there would be an overwhelmingly negative response or resistance to suggestions that this ministry should be revived and developed within the contemporary church. The results of the survey conducted as part of the thesis research were therefore both surprising and encouraging. Most respondents accepted that Christian discipline is a covenant responsibility and indicated support for its exercise, as long as they were satisfied as to the biblical basis of specific actions and that such actions were undertaken in humility, with compassion, and always in an effort to reconcile and restore individuals to one another and to the community of faith.

This book has been an effort to demonstrate the biblical bases for the practice of formative and reformative discipline, especially its warrant as a fundamental element of the covenant between and among believers, to discuss its broad outlines, and to provide some examples, positive and negative, of the practice of Christian discipline through history. It has also considered the legal issues and aspects of the culture which tend to deter churches from imposing disciplinary measures and made suggestions about the pillars on which church discipline might be based—first and foremost of course, the Bible, and then Statements of Faith and Church Covenants, Constitution and Bylaws or equivalent governance documents—as well as possibilities for specific disciplinary practices and processes, both formative and reformative.

At the heart of the argument in favor of Christian discipline has always been the paradigm offered in both the Older and New Testaments—i.e., that believers are members of a community bound together by a covenant. Reflecting on Howard Thurman's views of community, Luther Smith writes:

> Community is imprinted on every expression of life . . . God's signature [is] on everything in creation . . . [c]ommunity also functions as humanity's home. We are created for community. We are born for community . . . and depend upon it for survival. We are nurtured by community. This does not deny that people experience abandonment and abuse. But such experiences are a betrayal of the stronger and more persistent urge for care and whole-making. Community is a gift of God. We honor this gift when we live in community with respect and care for its members and all creation. Stewardship of community is thus a fundamental spiritual discipline. [To be committed] to the reconciling community is to know joy, renewal, and a sense of ultimate fulfillment. Frustration and disappointment remain, but they do not become the dominant emotions . . . the forces of love, cooperation, right relationship, respect and nurture will prevail.[1]

Whereas legalism simply passes judgment and metes out penalty, the covenant responsibility to practice Christian discipline seeks, through love, to nurture mutual member care to prevent spiritual lapses and to gently but firmly seek to encourage repentance and changed behavior in order that the erring one might be restored to his or her rightful place in the body of Christ. In a constantly changing world, the church must remain flexible and open to adapting or updating its methods and specific practices; however, as an institution built on clear absolutes, its principles are constant and must remain non-negotiable. One such principle is that of the covenant responsibility to practice discipline in the community of faith.

Consequently, Christian discipline, both formative and reformative, must be preserved and practiced rather than discarded or ignored as a vestige of unenlightened times by the promoters of modernity or post-modernity, or because of a "growth-and-unity-at-any-cost" philosophy. On the contrary, if Christian discipline is indeed called for in the community of faith, then even as the health and growth of the human body depends on wholesome habits (namely, the disciplines of eating, exercise, etc.), so too will Christian discipline, both formative and corrective, serve to nurture church health and growth. To discard and neglect the practice of discipline, on the other hand, will surely result in (even more) spiritual chaos and a further deterioration of the body of Christ.

1. Smith, *Howard Thurman: Essential Writings*, 88–91.

As was stated so clearly in Judges: "In those days there was no king in Israel; every man did what was right in his own eyes" (Judg 21:25). Where Christ is Lord, however, and his word law, there is liberty, through the Spirit, for the obedient! Would that the standards established by Jesus might guide our conduct so that collectively the church will become salt and light in a morally confused and confusing age. If it is to accomplish this, the church must boldly rise to accept Yahweh's challenging invitation to his people, Israel: "Awake, awake; put on your strength, O Zion; put on your beautiful garments, O Jerusalem, the holy city; from henceforth there shall no more come into you the uncircumcised and the unclean. Shake yourself from the dust, arise, O captive Jerusalem; loose the bonds from your neck, O captive daughter of Zion" (Isa 52:1,2).

Christian discipline can and must be more than mere legalism. It is a ministry that declares that Christians are their brothers' and sisters' keepers, and that all are under a divine mandate to teach and preach the "whole counsel of God." An integral part of that mandate, Christian discipline is both a covenant responsibility and a privilege to be exercised fully and forthrightly in the community of faith. It is a ministry of pastoral care and, when exercised with integrity and openness, it has the potential to encourage the believers and help them to "bear one another's burdens," for the benefit of individual believers and the community and to the glory of God.

Where churches fail to practice discipline, the reputation of the gospel is undermined; God's own attitude toward it is ignored; and the body of the church is contaminated. On the other hand, when the church practices Christian discipline, in love, and with reconciliation and restoration as its goals, the credibility and vitality of the church both increase and, most important, the gospel is honored. As Dietrich Bonhoeffer writes: "Words of admonition and reproach must be risked."[2]

---

2. Ortberg, "Spheres of Accountability," 33–34.

Bibliography

Arndt, W. F., and F. W. Gingrich. *A Greek-English Lexicon of the New Testament and other Early Christian Literature*. 4th ed. Chicago: University of Chicago Press, 1957.
Attridge, Harold W. *The Epistle to the Hebrews*. Edited by Helmut Koester. Philadelphia, PA: Fortress, 1989.
Baker, Don. *Beyond Forgiveness: The Healing Touch of Church Discipline*. Portland, OR: Multnomah, 1984.
Barclay, William. *The Daily Study Bible: The Letter to the Corinthians*. Edinburgh: The Saint Andrew Press, 1975.
Bauer, Walter. *Paideia*, in *A Greek-English Lexicon of the New Testament and other Early Christian Literature*. Translated and adapted by W.F. Arndt and F.W. Gingrich. Chicago: University of Chicago Press, 1957.
Behm, J., and G. Quelle, "*Diathēkē*" in *Theological Dictionary of the New Testament*. Edited by Gerhard Kittel. Translated by G.W. Bromiley. Vol. 4. Grand Rapids, MI: Eerdmans, 1964.
Bellah, Robert N., et al. *Habits of the Heart*. New York: Harper & Row, 1985.
Bertram, Georg, "*Paideia*" in *Theological Dictionary of the New Testament*. Edited by Gerhard Kittel. Translated by G.W. Bromiley. Vol. 5. Grand Rapids, MI: Eerdmans, 1964.
Bibby, Reginald. *Unknown Gods*. Toronto, ON: Stoddart, 1993.
Blaikie, David, and Diana Ginn. *The Legal Guide for Canadian Churches*. Ottawa, ON: Novalis, 2006.
Blamires, Harry. *The Christian Mind*. London: SPCK, 1963.
Blenkinsopp, Joseph. "Deuteronomy" in *The Jerome Biblical Commentary*. Edited by Raymond E. Brown, et al. Englewood Cliffs, NJ: Prentice-Hall, 1990.
Blum, Edwin A. "John." *Bible Knowledge Commentary: New Testament*. Edited by Walvoord and Zuck. Colorado Springs, CO: Cook Communication Ministries, 2004. 267–348.
Bounds, E. M. *The Essentials of Prayer*. Grand Rapids, MI: Christian Classics Ethereal Library, 2004.
Bright, John. *A History of Israel*. 3rd ed. Philadelphia, PA: Westminster, 1981.
Brown, Francis, et al. *Hebrew and English Lexicon of the Old Testament*. Oxford: Clarendon, 1906.
Bruce, F.F. *The Epistle to the Hebrews*. Grand Rapids, MI: Eerdmans, 1970.
Brueggemann, Walter. *Interpretation and Obedience*. Minneapolis: Fortress, 1991.
Buttrick, George A. "A Simple Regimen of Private Prayer" in *Devotional Classics*. Edited by Richard Foster and James Bryan Smith. New York: Renovare, 1993.
Burge, Gary M. "Gospel of John" in *The Bible Knowledge Background Commentary: John's Gospel, Hebrews–Revelation*. Edited by Craig A. Evans. Colorado Springs, CO: Cook Communications Ministries/Victor. 2005.

Byassee, Jason. "Dare to Discipline?" *Christian Century* 121.15 (2006), 8–9.
Calvin, John. *Commentary on the Epistles of Paul to the Corinthians*. Vol. I. Edinburgh: Calvin Translation Society, 1964.
Carson, D. A. "Matthew" in *The Expositor's Bible Commentary*. Edited by Frank E. Gaebelein. Vol. 8. Grand Rapids, MI: Zondervan, 1976–.
Carter, Harold A. *The Prayer Tradition of Black People*. Valley Forge, PA: Judson, 1976.
Carter, Terrance S. *A Legal Analysis of Church Discipline in Canada* and *Church Discipline Update*. 1995. Online: www.carters.ca/pub/article/church/1995/discplin.pdf.
Childs, Brevard S. *Biblical Theology of the Old and New Testaments*. Minneapolis, MN: Fortress, 1992.
———. "Canterbury Crackup." *Christianity Today*. (July 2005). Online: http://www.christianitytoday.com/ct/2005/august/13.31.html
Cram, Bill. "An Exploration of Church Membership Beliefs and Practices." A Study Paper submitted to the Faith, Order and Church Relations Committee of the Canadian Baptist Federation. (April 1990).
De Koster, L. "Church Discipline" in *Evangelical Dictionary of Theology*. Edited by Walter A. Ewell. Grand Rapids, MI: Baker, 1984.
Deweese, Charles. *A Community of Believers*. Valley Forge, PA: Judson Press, 1978.
Dumbrell, W.J. *Covenant and Creation*. Exeter: Paternoster, 1984.
Eichrodt, Walter. *Theology of the Old Testament*. Translated by J.A. Bakker. Philadelphia, PA: Westminster, 1961.
Ellis, David J. "The Gospel According to John" in *The New Layman's Bible Commentary*. Edited by G. C. D. Howley, et al. Grand Rapids, MI: Zondervan, 1979.
Foster, Richard. *Study Guide for Celebration of Discipline*. San Francisco: Harper & Row, 1983.
Fowler, James. *Stages of Faith*. San Francisco: Harper Collins, 1981.
Furst, D. "*Paideuō*." *Dictionary of New Testament Theology*, Vol. 3. Edited by Colin Brown. Exeter: Paternoster, 1978. 775–781.
Gaventa, Beverly. "Costly Confrontation." *Christian Century*. 110.23 (August 1993) 773.
Gibbs, Jeffrey. *Concordia Commentary: Matthew 11:2–20:34*, St. Louis, MO: Concordia, 2010.
Groome, Thomas H. *Christian Religious Education*. San Francisco: Harper & Row, 1980.
Ghurt, Joachim. "*Diathēkē*," *Dictionary of New Testament Theology*. Edited by Colin Brown. Vol. 1. Grand Rapids, MI: Zondervan, 1971.
Harrison, Everett F. "Romans" in *The Expositor's Bible Commentary*. Edited by Frank E. Gaebelein. Vol. 10. Grand Rapids, MI: Zondervan, 1976–.
Hauerwas, Stanley. "Discipleship as a Craft, Church as a Disciplined Community." *Christian Century*. 108 (October 1991) 881–84.
Hestenes, Roberta. "Can Spiritual Maturity Be Taught?" *Leadership*. 9.4 (Fall 1988)12–20.
Hillers, Delbert. *Covenant: The History of a Biblical Idea*. Baltimore, MD: Johns Hopkins, 1969.
Hughes, Philip E. *A Commentary on the Epistle to the Hebrews*. Grand Rapids, MI: Eerdmans, 1977.
Jeschke, Marlin. *Discipling in the Church: Recovering a Ministry of the Gospel*. 3rd. ed., rev., Scottsdale, AZ: Herald, 1988.
Jeschke, Marlin. "How Discipline Died." *Christianity Today*, (August 2005).

Julian of Norwich. "The Highest Form of Prayer" in *Devotional Classics*. Edited by Richard Foster and James Bryan Smith. New York: HarperCollins, 2005. 77.

Kilpatrick, William. *Why Johnny Can't Tell Right From Wrong*. New York: Simon & Schuster, 1992.

Laney, J. Carl. "Church Discipline Without a Lawsuit." *Christianity Today*. 28.16 (November 1984) 76.

LaSor, William S, et al. *Old Testament Survey*. Grand Rapids, MI: Eerdmans, 1982.

Liddell, Henery G., and Robert Scott. *A Greek-English Lexicon*. New York: Harper and Brothers, 1889.

Manetsch, Scott M. "Pastoral Care East of Eden: The Consistory of Geneva, 1568–82." *Church History*. 75.02. (2006) 312–13.

McComiskey, Thomas E. *The Covenants of Promise*. Grand Rapids, MI: Baker, 1985.

McDonald, Lee. Martin, "Introduction to I Corinthians" in *The Bible Knowledge Background Commentary: Acts–Philemon*. Colorado Springs, CO: Cook Communications Ministries/Victor. 2004.

Mell, Patrick H. *Corrective Church Discipline*. Paris, AR: Southern Baptist Publication Society, 1860.

Miles, John. *The History of The Chester Baptist Church: 1811–1907 -96 Years*. Publication Information Unknown.

Miller, Kevin. "Church Discipline for Repetitive Sin." *Leadership*. (Spring 2009) 39–41.

Morris, Leon. "Hebrews" in *The Expositor's Bible Commentary*. Edited by Frank E. Gaebelein. Vol. 12. Grand Rapids, MI: Zondervan, 1981.

Moulton, J. H., and G. Milligan. *The Vocabulary of the Greek Testament*. London: Hodder and Stoughton, 1952.

Murray, Stuart Eldon. *Through Him Who Strengthens Me: Selected Shorter Writings and Sermons*. Hantsport, NS: Lancelot Press, 1989.

Neff, David. "Healing the Body of Christ" in "Views on Church Discipline." *Christianity Today*. August 2005. Online: http://www.christianitytoday.com/ct/2005/august/19.34.html.

Neil, William. *The Epistle to the Hebrews*. London: SCM, 1955.

Nicoll, W. Robertson., ed. *The Expositor's Greek Testament*. London: Hodder & Stoughton, 1910.

Oepke, A. "Sickness and Sin" and "The Church and Sickness" in *Theological Dictionary of the New Testament*. Edited by G. Kittel. Translated by G.W. Bromiley. Vol. 4. Grand Rapids, MI: Eerdmans, 1967.

Ortberg, John. "Spheres of Accountability" in "Views on Church Discipline." *Christianity Today*. August 2005.

Payne, Barton J. *Theology of the Older Testament*. Grand Rapids, MI: Zondervan, 1962.

Pfeiffer, Charles F. and Everett F. Harrison, eds. "The Gospel According to John" in *The Wycliffe Bible Commentary*. Nashville: The Southwestern Company, 1962.

Price, Tom. "Church Discipline and Reconciliation." *Christian Century*. 109 (August 1992). 702–3.

Rambo, Lewis. "Interview with Reverend Marie Fortune, August 8, 1990." *Pastoral Psychology*. 39.5 (1991) 305–19.

Rienecker, Fritz, and Cleon Rogers. *Linguistic Key to the Greek New Testament*. Grand Rapids, MI: Zondervan, 1976.

Sande, Ken. "Keeping the Lawyers at Bay" in "Views on Church Discipline." *Christianity Today* (August 2005) 34–35.

Bibliography

Selter, F. "Exhort" in *Dictionary of New Testament Theology*. Vol. I. Grand Rapids, MI: Zondervan, 1975.

Shires, Henry H., and Peirson Parker. "Deuteronomy" in *Interpreters Bible Commentary*. Edited by G.A. Buttrick. Vol. 2. New York: Abingdon, 1953.

Shults, F. Leron and Steven J. Sandage, *Transforming Spirituality*. Grand Rapids, MI: Baker, 2006.

Smith, Luther E., Jr. *Howard Thurman: Essential Writings*. Maryknoll, NY: Orbis, 2006.

Sommer, Elisabeth. "A Different Kind of Freedom? Order and Discipline among the Moravian Brethren in Germany and Salem, North Carolina 1771–1801." *Church History*. 63 (June 1994) 221–27.

Steere, Douglas V. "*The Inner Springs Of Prayer*" in *Devotional Classics*. Edited by Richard Foster and James Bryan Smith. New York: Renovare, 1993, 88.

Stibbs, A. M. "*Paideia*" in *The New Bible Commentary Revised*. Edited by D. Guthrie, et al. Grand Rapids, MI: Eerdmans, 1970.

Stott, John. *Confess Your Sins: The Way of Reconciliation*. London: Hodder & Stoughton, 1964.

Tamney, Joseph B. "Does Strictness Explain the Appeal of Working-Class Conservative Protestant Congregations?" *Sociology of Religion*, Fall 2005, 283–302.

Tennyson, Alfred North. "Morte d'Arthur." *The Norton Anthology of English Literature*. 4th ed. Toronto: Norton, 1979.

Underhill, Evelyn. "What Do We Mean By Prayer?" in *Devotional Classics*. Edited by Richard Foster and James Bryan Smith. New York: Renovare, 1993.

Vitz, Paul C. *Psychology as Religion*. Grand Rapids, MI: Eerdmans, 1977.

Vos, Geerhardus. "Hebrews, Epistle of the *Diathēkē*." *Princeton Theological Review*. 13. (1915), 587–634.

Wessel, Walter W. "Mark" in *The Expositor's Bible Commentary*. Edited by Frank E. Gaebelein. Vol. 8. Grand Rapids, MI: Zondervan, 1976–.

Westcott, Brooke Foss. *Epistle to the Hebrews*. London: Macmillan, 1909.

White, Mervyn F. and Suzanne E. White. "Recent Decision Casts Doubt on Use of Matthew 18: 15–18 to Address Church Disputes." Carters Professional Corporation *Church Law Bulletin*. 3 (April 2004) Online http://www.carters.ca/pub/bulletin/church/2004/chchlb03.htm

White, Suzanne E. *Fair Play in Action—Towards Effective Discipline within the Church*. Carters Professional Corporation. The 2007 Annual Church & Charity Law™ Seminar, Toronto, November 7, 2007. Online: http://www.carters.ca/pub/seminar/chrchlaw/ott/08/jbr0206.pdf

Willard, Dallas. *Renovation of the Heart: Putting on the Character of Christ*. Colorado Springs, CO: NavPress, 2002.

Wilson, R. McL. *The New Century Bible Commentary: Hebrews*. Grand Rapids, MI: Eerdmans, 1987.

Wray, Daniel. *Biblical Church Discipline*. Carlisle, PA: The Banner of Truth Trust, 1978.

Yancey, Philip. *Prayer: Does It Make Any Difference?* Grand Rapids, MI: Zondervan, 2006.

Youngblood, Ronald. *Heart of the Old Testament*. Grand Rapids, MI: Baker, 1971.

Zander, Dieter, and Dallas Willard. "The Apprentices." *Leadership*. 26.3 (Summer 2005) 20–25.

Scripture Index

Genesis

9	10
9:9	10
21:21–32	10n2
21:31–32	10
26:26–33	10n2
26:28–29	10

Exodus

4:22	100
12:15	25
13:3, 7	25
18	113
19:5–6	22
24:5–8	25
24:8	25

Leviticus

20:10	3
26	16
26:1–20	19
26:40–46	19
26:23	2n4

Deuteronomy

6:1–7	90
6:6–7	16
6:20–25	14
7:6–15	11
8	16
8:1–6	16
8:1–5	19
8:3	16, 122
8:5	17
8:6	16
11:2	16, 17
16:3	25
21:18–22	17
21:21	18
22:18–22	19
22:18	17
22:22–24	3
29	17
30:15–20	12

Joshua

7	19, 28, 32

Judges

21:25	127

1 Kings

5:12	10

Job

4:3	57
23:15	57
34:16	57
36:12	57
37:14	57
38:18	57

Scripture Index

Psalms

19:7–11	122
24	99
94:10, 12	18, 19
118:18	18
119:9–11	99
119:11, 104	122
119:11	90

Proverbs

1:1	17
2:1–11	122
2:1	20
2:5–13	20
8:33	17

Isaiah

1:2	100
42:1–4	100
51:13–53:12	25
52:1, 2	127
53:5	2n4
61:1–11	23

Jeremiah

29:10, 11	9
29:12–14	21
31:31–34	23, 24, 25
31:34	25

Ezekiel

16:8	13
16:32	13
18:32	15
36:21–38	23
36:26–27	23

Daniel

1–4	122

Hosea

2:19–20	13
11:1	100
14:3	100

Amos

3:1–8	19
3:2	18, 31

Zechariah

9:11	25

Matthew

4:4	122
5:17	26
9:1–8	7
13	7
13:19–23	7
13:24–33	7
13:47–50	7
16:18	36
16:19	27, 48
16:21–28	28
17:22, 23	28
18	36, 44, 62, 79, 80, 81, 82, 55
18:1–10	55
18:1–5	28
18:7–14	7
18:12–14	4, 55
18:15–22	4, 55, 56
18:15–20	87, 94, 95
18:15–18	48, 49, 55n4, 80, 81, 82, 83
18:15–17	6, 57, 63
18:15	49, 55, 59, 94
18:16, 18	82
18:17	4, 49, 65, 82

Scripture Index

18:18	27	8:11	3
18:19–20	55n4	10	25
18:21–35	7	15	122
18:22	4	15:1–5	123
18:23–35	4, 56, 82	15:3	99
20:20–28	28	15:15	100
26:26–28	20	16:21–24	43
26:28	25	17:6, 8, 14, 17, 20	122
26:41	6	21:23	48
28:19–20	27, 42		

Mark

Acts

		2:37–47	101
2:3–12	7	2:46	25
2:5 ff	5	4:29–31	101
7	23	5	28, 32
7:20–23	23	5:1–11	94
10:35–45	28	5:1–10	101
10:43–44	100	7:22	28
14:24	20, 25	15:1–35	58
		20:31	57
		22:3	28, 30

Luke

5:18–26	7	
7:36–50	7	
11	49	
15:11–32	61	
15:18	49	
17:3	117	
22:20	25	
23:16, 22	28	

Romans

2:23–24	60
3:21, 22	23
12–16	99
12–13	101
12	104
12:1–2	96, 99, 122
12:1	100n4
12:2	99
12:4–13	101
12:7–10	49
12:14	101
12:15–16	101
12:17–18	101
12:19–21	101
13	101
14:1–15:13	101
15:14	57

John

1:1, 14	122
1:12	20, 30, 100
1:29	25
3:3–5	99
3:3, 5	30
6:63–69	122
8	4, 5
8:1–11	3
8:5	3
8:7b	3

Scripture Index

1 Corinthians

4:14	57
5	5, 32, 59
5:1–11	6
5:1–5	63, 94
5:2	6
5:2b	60
5:3–5	49
5:4–5	30
5:4b-8	60
5:5	94
5:6–8	92, 95
5:6	5
5:7	60
5:12–13	6
5:12	49
6:1–11	84
10	32, 58
10:1–13	49
10:11	57
10:16–17	25
11:17–34	64
11:27–32	23
11:25	25
11:32	28, 30
12	76, 104
12:3	23
12:24–26	5
12:28	49

2 Corinthians

2	5
2:5–11	59
2:6–11	49
2:6–8	6
2:8	95
2:10–11	6
4:17	30
5:17–21	99
6:9	28, 30
12:1	100
12:7	30

Galatians

3:6–9	26
3:12	23
3:15–17	26
3:26–27	20
4:1–7	100
4:4–7	26
5	122
6:1–10	36
6:1–5	59
6:1, 2	95
6:1	59, 95, 117

Ephesians

2	86
4	36, 58, 122
4:11–16	58
4:11	113
6:4	57

Philippians

3	122

Colossians

1:28	57, 58
3:1–17	100
3:16	57

1 Thessalonians

5:12, 14	57
5:14	94

2 Thessalonians

2:14	49
3:6–15	94
3:15	57, 95

1 Timothy

1 Tim	58
1:20	28, 30
5:17	49
5:19–22	82
5:20	94, 95

2 Timothy

2 Tim	58
2:25	28, 30

Titus

1:13	94
2:12	28, 30
3:10	57, 94

Hebrews

1:3	xvi
8:6–13	22
9:15	22
9:16–17	24
9:17–19	27
10:24–25	58
12:4–13	32
12:5–11	29
12:6, 10	30
12:7–12	20
12:7, 10	28, 30
12:9, 10	30
12:9	20
12:10–11	95

James

1:18, 21–22	122
4:4	13n15
5:16	57

1 Peter

2	86
2:4–10	31
2:5	22
9–11	22

2 Peter

1:1–11	111

1 John

1:8	5

Jude

5–13	60

Revelation

1:5	30
2–3	62, 94
3:9, 19	30
3:19	28, 30

Subject Index

A

abuse, 69, 77, 79, 80, 80n27, 81, 83–84, 90, 126
abuse of church discipline, 33
accountable, 19, 36, 39, 41, 51, 58, 66, 76, 86, 90, 93
accountability, xvi, 34–35, 39, 47, 56, 76, 86, 95, 100–101, 103–105, 113, 115
action (disciplinary), 5–6, 18, 30, 34, 36, 39–41, 50, 57, 59, 66, 69, 70, 73, 75, 83, 94, 108, 115–118, 120, 121, 125
admonition, 5–7, 18, 28, 30–31, 37–38, 40, 44–46, 48, 50, 57–58, 64, 66, 76, 127
Anabaptist(s), 103
Atlantic Canada, ix, xvi, 36

B

Baptist(s), ix, 36, 49–50, 53, 103–104
believer(s), vii, 22–24, 26, 28, 30, 33, 35, 38, 41, 48, 54, 56–59, 62–63, 66–67, 76, 86, 89, 91, 93–94, 96, 98, 100–105, 112–113, 122, 125, 127
Bible, xiv, 22, 36, 38, 40, 42, 89, 98, 106, 111, 113, 123, 125
board (of elders or deacons), xiii, xiv, 46, 69, 107, 116, 117, 118
bona fide occupational requirement, 73, 74

C

Calvin, xvi, 34, 45, 47
celebration, ix, 61, 95, 121
chastise(ment), 1–2, 2n4, 18, 18n34, 19, 28–29
child abuse, 81, 83
children, xv, xvi, 4, 7, 16, 20, 29–32, 55, 74, 77, 83, 91, 100
Christian discipline, vii, viii, ix, x, xiv, xv, xvi, xvii, 1–3, 5–10, 31, 33, 35–39, 41–44, 48–50, 53–56, 59, 61, 66–69, 71–73, 75, 77, 79, 81, 85–86, 89, 91–93, 95, 97–99, 101–103, 106–108, 111–113, 115, 120–121, 123, 125–127
Christian education, 91
Church Covenant, 67, 101–105, 107, 111, 125
church discipline, xv, 2, 8, 22n1, 33–34, 45–48, 48n11, 57n7, 57n8, 59n15, 60n19, 61, 61n23, 63, 67, 67n3, 70–71, 71n7, 72, 73n13, 75n15, 75n16, 76, 76n19, 77, 77n20, 77n21, 94, 102n10, 103, 103n12, 104n21, 106n25, 109, 116, 120n14
church membership, xiv, 33, 102, 104n18, 105, 109
clergy, 71n10, 73–74, 77, 81–83, 109, 115
community, vii, viii, 2–6, 8, 17–20, 24–25, 29, 31, 33–34, 36–37, 41–43, 46–47, 50–51, 55, 57–60, 62, 67, 74, 76, 80, 84, 86–91, 93, 101–104, 106, 112–114, 121, 125–127
community actualization, 88
compassionate formation, 8

Subject Index   139

conduct, xiv, 1–2, 4, 6, 12, 17, 22, 34–35, 37, 41, 45–47, 49–50, 57, 83, 93, 98, 100, 103, 110, 117–118, 125, 127
confession, ix, 30, 46, 49, 57, 90, 95, 119, 121
confidential(ity), 76–77, 117, 120
congregation(s), vii–x, xiii–xvi, 2, 5–6, 8, 29, 33–36, 39–40, 42, 42n8, 43–44, 46, 49, 49n13, 50–51, 53–54, 58, 62, 66, 71, 76, 82, 90, 92–94, 102–103, 105–107, 112–113, 116, 119, 123
Constitution and Bylaws, 67, 72, 104, 106–108, 111, 125
correction, xv–xvi, 8, 17, 19, 28–30, 37, 50, 54, 57–58
corrective (discipline), 7, 29, 39, 62, 92, 95
covenant, vii–ix, xv–xvii, 4, 10, 10n1–2, 11, 11n3, 12, 12n9, 12n11, 13, 13n15, 13n16, 14, 14n21, 15, 18–22, 22n2, 23, 23n3–4, 24, 24n7, 25, 25n10, 26, 26n11, 26n17, 27, 27n19–20, 29, 31–33, 36, 40–41, 49–50, 54–55, 62–63, 67, 72, 74, 95, 101–103, 103n13, 104–111, 113, 115, 125–127
covenant responsibility, ix, xvi, 49, 125–127
culture, x, xv–xvi, 45, 53, 57, 61, 86–87, 90–91, 96, 98–100, 112, 122, 125

D

defamation (of character), 75–78, 78n22, 79
discipleship, vii, 7, 34–36, 87n1, 89, 91, 95, 103, 119
disciplinary action, 5, 36, 39–40, 50, 66, 69, 73, 83, 115–118, 120
disciplinary practices, 34, 44–45, 96, 125
disciplinary process(es), 68, 71, 93–94, 115
discipline (Christian), vii, viii, ix, x, xiv, xv, xvi, xvii, 1–3, 5–10, 31, 33, 35–39, 41–44, 48–50, 53–56, 59, 61, 66–69, 71–73, 75, 77, 79, 81, 85–86, 89, 91–93, 95, 97–99, 101–103, 106–108, 111–113, 115, 120–121, 123, 125–127
discrimination, 38, 73
divine-human relationship, 6, 20, 24, 31
due process (*See* duty of fairness), 68, 70, 109
duty of fairness, 68–71, 85, 109

E

early church, xvi, 44, 53
elders, 8, 17, 18, 45–48, 69, 75–76, 79–82, 107, 116, 120
employment law, 71, 71n9–10, 72n11
exclusion, xiv, 46, 50–51, 55, 62, 72, 122
excommunication, 2, 18, 20, 30, 33, 38, 40–41, 46–48, 49n13, 59–62, 65, 67, 69, 71

F

faith community, 17, 20, 57, 59, 60, 89, 93, 103, 113
faith(ful)(ness), ix, x, 5, 7–8, 11–13, 13n15, 15, 17, 20, 22–24, 26–27, 29–31, 36, 38–39, 42, 45, 49–50, 55–57, 59–60, 62, 68, 72, 73, 74, 79, 88–89, 91–93, 96, 98, 100–111, 113–114, 114n9, 115, 121–122, 125–127
fear, x, xvi, 5, 14, 16–17, 19, 28, 38, 54, 66–67, 76, 95
fellowship, xiii, xiv, 6–7, 20, 22, 30–31, 34, 45–46, 50–52, 55n4, 56–60, 62, 66, 76, 87, 92, 94, 103–104, 113, 115, 117, 120
formation (spiritual), vii, 45, 47–48, 91, 98, 112, 121–122
formative discipline, 14, 27, 29, 31, 37, 56, 101, 104, 112
freedom(s) (personal), xvi, 13, 32, 87n2, 89

G

Geneva, xvi, 8, 34–35, 45–48, 53
gospel(s), 3, 3n7–8, 5n10, 7, 24, 33n1, 35–36, 44, 48–49, 51, 55, 59, 61, 88, 100, 114, 127
guidance, ix, 6, 8, 30, 37, 48, 81, 121

H

harassment, 69, 79
human rights (law, complaint, legislation), xvi, 72–73, 72n11, 73n12, 79

I

impediments (to Christian discipline), 92–93
implementation (of discipline), 34, 97, 108
individualism, xv, xvi, 41, 76, 86–87, 89, 98–99, 104, 112
individual rights, 67, 86, 89
intervention, 15, 47–48, 110, 114
invasion of privacy, 76, 79
Israel, 11–12, 12n4–5, 13–17, 19, 23, 27, 31, 58, 127

J

judgmental, xiv, 38, 86
judicial review, 69–70, 70n6, 71, 79

L

law (lawsuit), xviii2, 1, 3, 3n7, 16–17, 23, 26, 34–35, 47, 50, 66, 66n1, 67–69, 71, 71n9–10, 72, 72n10–11, 73, 75–76, 76n19, 77, 78n22, 79–81, 85, 98, 106, 106n24–25, 108–109, 115, 116, 127
lay leader(s), xiv, 73, 109–110
legal (liability, action), xvii, 11, 22, 41, 66, 66n1, 67, 67n3, 68–70, 71n7, 71n9, 72, 72n10, 73n13, 75, 75n15–16, 76–77, 77n20–21, 78, 78n22, 79, 81n28, 85, 98, 102n10, 103, 104n21, 107, 78n22, 108, 110, 115, 117, 119–120, 125
legalism, ix, 34–35, 43, 125
litigation, 96
love, 6, 11, 13–17, 20–21, 25, 29–32, 35–37, 39, 42, 55n4, 60–61, 64, 87–88, 93–95, 105, 110, 113, 115, 120n14, 126–127

M

maturity (spiritual), 36, 112, 112n1, 113, 113n4
member subject to discipline (subject member), 116–118
member(s) (ship), xiii–xvi, 1–5, 19–20, 29, 31, 33–41, 46–47, 49–51, 54–55, 55n4, 57–60, 62–63, 66–69, 71–72, 72n10, 73–78, 80n27, 81–83, 86–87, 89–90, 93, 95, 102–104, 104n18, 105, 108–109, 115–121, 125–126
ministry (of Christian discipline), xvi, 2, 86, 95, 98, 101, 107, 108, 111
mutual accountability, xvi, 47, 76, 86, 103, 113

N

negligence, 75, 79–80, 82
negligent counseling, 83
New Testament, xvi, 5n9, 7n11, 12n4, 13n15, 20, 22, 24–25, 25n8, 26–28, 28n23, 29n25, 30–31, 31n33, 32, 55n5, 57, 57n9, 58, 76, 99, 100n3, 102, 125

O

obedience, xv, 1, 11–13, 13n15, 14–17, 19, 23–26, 26n17, 27, 29, 31, 47, 56, 71, 87–88, 100, 100n5

Older Testament, 10, 10n2, 14–16, 18, 22–23, 25–26, 27n19, 28, 30–31
operational guidelines, 67, 107

P

parents, xv, 16–17, 31–32, 90–91
pastor(s), xiii–xiv, 2, 4, 8, 36, 39–40, 45, 47–48, 57–59, 64, 72n10, 74–76, 81, 83, 90–91, 93–94, 97, 107, 109–110, 113–114, 119–120, 123
pastoral care, xiii, xiv, 2, 8, 8n12, 45, 45n2, 47–48, 82–83, 113, 127
personal transformation, 114
practice(s), vii, ix–x, xv–xvii, 1–3, 6–9, 20, 27, 27n20, 28, 30, 33–36, 42–45, 47–49, 49n13, 50–51, 53, 62, 66, 81, 82, 84–86, 92, 94, 96–98, 100–103, 103n18, 106–108, 111, 113, 115, 121–123, 125–127
prayer, ix, 9n13, 21, 32n34, 38, 40, 43, 51, 53, 53n22, 57, 64, 64n29, 84n33, 88, 96, 96n28, 111n27, 113, 119, 121
prevention, xv–xvi, 6
principle(s)(of Christian discipline), vii, xiv, 5, 7–8, 14, 18–19, 31–32, 41, 47, 49, 53, 58, 59, 66n1, 67–68, 87, 89–91, 93, 98, 101, 104–106, 108–109, 113, 117, 126
punishment, 1–2, 6, 15, 18–19, 29–32, 47, 80
Puritans, 103

R

reconcile, reconciled, reconciliation, xiii, 4, 6, 10, 16, 50, 57n7, 59, 65, 105, 115, 119, 121, 125–127
redemptive transformation, 114
reformative (discipline), 10, 14–16, 19, 28, 36–37, 56, 92, 104, 112, 115–116, 125
relationship, xiii–xvi, 1, 4, 6, 10, 10n2, 11–15, 17–25, 25n11, 26–27, 29–34, 48, 54–55, 55n4, 56, 59, 61–62, 64, 72–73, 76, 85, 95, 101, 103, 114, 126
repentance, xiv, xv, 4, 7–8, 12–13, 19, 28, 30, 37, 39–40, 46, 48, 50, 55n4, 59–60, 62, 67, 95, 114, 126
responsibility, vii, ix, xvi, 4, 29, 34, 37, 49, 55n4, 58, 61, 90–92, 101, 104, 113, 125–127
restore, restoration, restorative (fellowship), vii, ix, xii–xvi, 4, 6–8, 10, 13–14, 16, 27–31, 35, 40, 44–48, 49n13, 51–52, 55, 55n4, 56, 59–60, 62–63, 65–67, 90, 93–95, 105, 114–115, 117, 119–121, 123, 125–127
retention, 55, 57
risk management, xvii, 115

S

screening, 79
secular courts, 66–67, 69–71, 74, 82, 118n12
Separatists (London), 103
sin(s)(ner(s))(ning)(ful), xvi, 2–8, 11, 18–25, 27–28, 30–31, 35, 37–39, 41, 44–49, 54–57, 57n8, 58–60, 62–65, 66n2, 67, 76n18, 81–82, 88–89, 94–95, 110, 119, 120n14, 122
spiritual disciplines, 119, 121–123, 126
spiritual formation, vii, 45, 47–48, 91, 98, 112, 121–122
spiritual maturity, 36, 112, 112n1, 113, 113n4
spiritual reflection, 6
spiritual reformation, 119
spiritual transformation, 98–99, 113–114, 122–123
standard(s) of behavior, xv, 6–8, 17, 20, 23, 35, 37, 42, 45, 47–48, 58, 61, 68–75, 90, 93, 98, 103–104, 109, 115, 120, 127
Statement of Faith, 72, 74, 102, 104, 106–111, 115

Statement of Mission and Identity, 102, 104, 106–108, 110–111, 115
subject member, 116–118
submission, ix, 23, 27, 47, 86–87, 99–100, 118, 121–122
systemic transformation, 114

T

training, xvi, 1–2, 8, 28n24, 30, 32, 57, 66, 86, 89
tort law, 75, 108

V

vicarious liability, 80

W

warrant (biblical), xv, 8, 33, 36, 67, 102, 125
Western culture, xv, 86, 90, 98–99
worship, ix, xiii, 2, 34, 42, 57, 63, 92, 103, 105, 113, 118–119, 121

www.ingramcontent.com/pod-product-compliance
Lightning Source LLC
Chambersburg PA
CBHW072203160426
43197CB00012B/2511

Entre l'orature et l'écriture
Relations croisées

Edité par

Charles Zacharie Bowao

et

Shahid Rahman

Préface de
Christian Berner et Marcel Nguimbi

© Individual authors and College Publications 2014
All rights reserved.

ISBN 978-1-84890-029-5

College Publications
Scientific Director: Dov Gabbay
Managing Director: Jane Spurr

http://www.collegepublications.co.uk

Printed by Lightning Source, Milton Keynes, UK

All rights reserved. No part of this publication may be reproduced, stored in a retrieval system or transmitted in any form, or by any means, electronic, mechanical, photocopying, recording or otherwise without prior permission, in writing, from the publisher.